MW01234973

THE PRODIGAL SON: THE ADDICT

Prod·i·gal */prädəg(ə)l/ Spending money or resources freely and recklessly; wastefully extravagant.*

Thomas Carr

Copyright

Acknowledgements

I would like to take this opportunity to thank the countless number of family and friends that have prayerfully supported me throughout my journey. Without you, my life would be meaningless.

My wife and children have also played a huge part in supporting me on this journey. Your endless support and encouragement along the way has meant more to me than words can ever describe.

Pastor Whit, thank you for sharing your time with me and for being there when I needed you most. Your guidance and support have encouraged me throughout my journey, and I am forever grateful for your friendship.

Benny & Annette, you will never fully understand what an impact our short time together had on me early on in my journey. The seeds that you planted in my early teenage years were fundamental in my journey home. Memories that I reflected back on from better times helped to lighten the stress of a darker place.

And lastly, I would like to thank my parents from the very core of my heart for always believing in me when I didn't believe in myself.

Table of Contents

Introduction

It was April 3, 1987, and just another Friday night of clubbing was planned at the usual nightclub. I stopped by the convenience store to grab a six-pack of Michelob beer and some smokes and then went to pick up Joey from work after his shift ended. He had already met up with his guy and scored an eight ball of coke for the night, and while I waited for his shift to end, I helped cut it and split it up into grams and half grams to sell to recoup the cost and then planned to party with the rest as we did most every weekend.

Little did we know, the Lexington drug task force had Joey and his workplace staked out and obviously knew of the activity going on there for some time. After getting everything bagged up, we did a few bumps to get started, picked a nice chunk out to tuck in our gums, and then as his shift ended, we headed out for the club.

As we pulled out onto the road, oblivious to the fact that we were being watched and now followed, we drove a block or so to the red light and hadn't any more come to a stop when both doors of the truck flew open, and we both were pulled from the vehicle. I could feel the cold steel barrel of what obviously was a gun placed to the side of my neck as I heard the officer say, "Get out of the truck, keep your mouth shut, and don't even breathe."

In total surprise and complete shock, it didn't take long to realize what was going on and that this was serious. More pissed off than anything that my buzz was shot, and even though the rock still in my lower gum hadn't yet fully dissolved, all I could do was just think of how screwed we both were.

They confiscated my truck and arrested us for trafficking in a controlled substance, and booked us into the Fayette County Detention Center. This was the old jail in Lexington, not the nice new facility they would soon build a few years later. This place was a nasty hell hole.

There was no way this was going to be kept quiet from my family as it had been with previous traffic stops and occasional nights in jail in the past for various other stupid stuff I had managed to get myself into.

It was the first time I was sure to spend real time in jail, and it just happened to be the same weekend my parents had gone away for a little vacation. I couldn't think of anyone I could call to try and bail me out, at least someone who wouldn't tell anyone what was happening. This wasn't my first run-in with the law, and it wouldn't be the last, but my family didn't necessarily know anything about it.

This wasn't how I was brought up, and I certainly knew better and was taught a much different way of life growing up. To get the full picture, I invite you to come along on this journey with me.

Chapter I

The Journey Begins (Childhood Years)

As we begin the journey, we will need to travel back in time to my childhood. I feel that it is important to get the whole story from the beginning to understand truly.

I was raised by loving Christian parents in a home where we always went to church every time the doors were open, and as a child, I never really had to want for anything. My parents weren't rich by any means, but they faced hardships and struggled to overcome difficult times during the Depression when things were much different than they are today.

As the youngest of four siblings, I was the baby, and according to my siblings, I was spoiled rotten. I didn't see it that way, of course; I just thought they loved me more than the others! Our parents always wanted the best for us and set a very good example for us growing up. We were taught the old-school biblical way. *"Train up a child in the way he should go: and when he is old, he will not depart from it." Proverbs 22:6*

My brother Jimmy was the oldest of us kids. He was sixteen years older than me, nearly old enough to be my dad. He was driving by the time I was even born. My sister Glenda was next in line, coming in at eight years older than me, and then there was my sister Jackie, who was closest to me at four years apart. Then there was me, the baby of the family.

Back then, there seemed to be a thing about having children four years apart. I guess they knew how to make it work for their best interest back then by having children far enough apart that they could help out with their younger siblings. There was also another girl in there between Jimmy and Glenda. Her name was Rosemary, but she was stillborn.

I've often wondered if she had lived, would Mom and Dad have stopped after four kids? My siblings always told me when I was growing up that I was an accident, so there's a very good chance that I would not have been born. I'm sure that they were so very happy when they got the exciting news of my unplanned existence.

We were loved beyond measure but disciplined when we needed it. We were never abused, but we endured the appropriate punishment when we did wrong. In my opinion, we all turned out to be pretty good people, and we tried to pass down those same values to our own children, but as with everything else in life, time changes the way you do things when it's your turn to be the parent.

I say this to get my point across that we knew right from wrong, and even though we knew better, we sometimes behaved like children and made mistakes. I was literally no exception to that rule. I had my share of punishment, even though I was the baby and spoiled rotten. Mom would always take up for me, which probably wasn't the best thing because it never really taught me that I had to be held accountable for my actions, and as I grew older, I never really knew what it meant to be held responsible for my actions.

While I often complained about spending so much time at church, it always seemed fun. There was always some kind of social, as they called it back then; a time when we, as southern Baptists, would get together for a potluck dinner. We didn't even need a special occasion or anything; we just celebrated everything. It was a big part of our life growing up, and we didn't really know it any other way.

Growing up, we weren't allowed to attend sock hops at school. Sock hops are dances for those of you that didn't know. This was the 50s and 60s, and people were a lot more conservative back then. Church folk just didn't spend time at the bars and nightclubs.

Instead, we had socials at the church fellowship hall, at church members' houses, at their farms, and just about anywhere and everywhere. Sometimes they included hayrides, sleigh rides, and bonfires. That's what made it so fun. It didn't seem like church to me at the time because I thought of church as the service part in the sanctuary on Sunday morning, Sunday night, and Wednesday night bible study.

Looking back now, I realize it was all church because the church isn't a service or a building; it's the body of believers coming together in fellowship with one another and serving Christ. I only wish that it meant as much to me then as the memories of it do to me now. I mean, yes, it was fun and probably some of the best times of my life, but I had no idea that those times would become memories that would be an everlasting timeline someday further down the road.

Mom sang in the choir, and Dad was a deacon and also served as an usher. Back then, the choir sat in the choir loft for the entire service, even the preaching. Mom would catch me misbehaving, make eye contact, and give me that look.

Just being present in church every week, even if I wasn't paying attention to the preacher's sermon, had an impact on me. The hymns that we sang each week were etched into my memory. I could recite at least the first verse of just about any hymn that we sang regularly. Little did I know back then what that would someday mean to me.

I can still recall my childhood years as if they were yesterday. My father was a residential home builder, and he would often take me with him around to the different job sites during the summer. My dad's brother and one of his nephews were all in the residential construction business together, and I had grown up around the business since my childhood, so Dad would often drop me off on one of the job sites for the day to get a feel of the business. From a very young age, I knew that's what I wanted to do when I got older.

The only friends I had outside of the church were my friends from our neighborhood. We lived on a cul-de-sac in Lexington, Kentucky, where I spent my entire childhood until I got married and moved out of the house for the first time.

There was me, Brad, Jeff, Sammy, Scott, and a few others from the neighboring subdivision, including Larry, Jason & Johnny. One of our moms referred to us as the 'Dead End Bunch' because we lived on the cul-de-sac and were almost always together as a team. We did everything together. We didn't have video games and cell phones back then, so we spent almost every day outside on some kind of adventure.

Like most mischievous kids during that time, we did our share of pranks on the neighborhood families, like ringing their doorbell, hiding in the bushes, and laughing at them when they came to the door only to find there wasn't anyone there. We sometimes would even leave them a paper bag with dog poop in it and set it on fire before we rang the doorbell, hoping they would come out and stomp out the fire only to smash the surprise all over their feet and the doorstep.

That wasn't anywhere near the only thing we did to get in trouble, but I'll just leave the rest of it for another time to not spark any ideas in the minds of anyone reading the story today. Even at our worst, we were never subjected to drugs like kids are in today's society. It was the 60s, and we were living our best life. The worst possible scenario was an occasional smoke that one of the guys would sneak from his old man's pack, and we would all share it, pretending to be cool, not having a clue what we were doing.

One of my favorite childhood memories was visiting our little farm in the nearby county. My father had purchased some land to develop into a subdivision, but he kept twelve acres in the back of the property and used it as a place to raise a garden, spend some family time away, and even raise a few horses. The memories of family reunions and church gatherings there on that farm remain some of my favorite memories even today.

I loved it there. As small as it was, to me, being the adventurous boy I was, it was like paradise. I mean, what young boy wouldn't like a place where he could explore nature, bareback on a pony, ride a mini dirt bike all over the farm, or play in the creek that ran the entire property?

One Saturday, while pulling into the farm with my dad, I got out to open the gate, and out of the corner of my eye, I noticed an unfamiliar person on our property. Someone was there with our horses, only more horses than usual. Well, at least one more, and there with the horses, stood this girl. Not just any girl, but a girl that appeared to be my age, with long blonde hair tied up in pigtails.

I was probably only about eight years old at the time, but until this point in life, girls had always been gross, and I wanted nothing to do with them. But for the first time, I was dumbfounded by her beauty. It was definitely one of those defining moments in a young boy's life.

My father explained that this was one of the people he had recently sold a house to in the neighborhood he was developing on the other side of our property. Their daughter had this pony, and she needed a place to keep it, so he agreed to let them keep it there on our farm with our other horses, and they agreed to keep an eye on our property and horses while we weren't there.

The fact that she just so happened to be my age was probably a coincidence, and maybe he didn't even know anything about her at the time, but as fate would have it, that little blonde-haired girl would one day become much more to me than just someone with a horse.

The more time we spent on the farm, the more I got to know her. It turned out that we shared birthdays. Not just shared them, but the exact same day, born just hours apart in the same hospital. I know, right? LeeAnne was her name, but her family called her Sissy. Needless to say, we spent even more time on the farm over the next several years, and the bond we built grew stronger over the years to come.

Chapter II

Early Teens (Early 1970's)

When I was 14, I remember my parents wanting me to join the youth group at our church. Our church had just hired a new minister of music, and he also served as a youth leader. They were rehearsing for a concert they planned to travel around and sing for other churches, and they were raising money for an upcoming summer trip to Florida. Mom thought it would be great if I went too, but I didn't want any part of it.

My parents thought it would be great for me to get involved in, but I didn't think that at all. We were already spending what seemed like every waking hour at church, and it seemed like I never had any time to just hang out with my friends. Joining a choir was the last thing on my radar, and at the time, it all just sounded weird to me, but my parents insisted I get involved. I agreed to give it a shot but wasn't making any promises.

It was 1972, and I was in the prime of my youth. I had already spent so much time as a child at church, and as a teenager, I was more interested in exploring my independence than hanging out at church. Needless to say, Mom won that disagreement, and the only way I was going on that Florida trip with the youth group was to start attending practices and at least try to learn some of the songs for the program.

The time came, and in the summer of 1974, Mom drove me to the church early one morning, dropped off me and my luggage, told me to behave myself and have a good time, and left. This was a totally new experience for me, and I was more than just a little uncomfortable, to say the least. However, my bonds with the entire group grew during this time. Mom knew that if she stuck around, I would probably talk her into not making me go.

Our group was called The Conquerors, and the concert we performed for the various churches along the way that summer was called 'The Touch of the Holy Spirit.' Benny and his wife, Annette, put it all together using a variety of different spiritual and gospel songs. Benny choreographed all of the songs, and Annette played the piano. Other members of the church helped with sound, lights, and instruments making it a church-wide effort.

It was not your usual choir performance. To open, we entered the sanctuary from all possible directions, clothed in all white while the music, "2001: A Space Odyssey", played. Remember that this was 1974, and the song was written in 1968, so it was well before the year 2001 and was not your typical song associated with the church, which made it even more unusual and grabbed your attention right from the beginning.

Benny and Annette were fresh out of college, and Benny was just beginning his career as a minister of music, and this performance would become one that moved a lot of people's hearts and turned many people to Christ over the years. It was unlike anything anyone had seen during the 70s.

I can remember one time in particular while we were in Florida. We were staying in a motel in one of the towns, and it just happened to be college spring break. Needless to say, partygoers were all over the place, and one evening, the college kids were all partying down by the pool. Benny, being the risk taker that he was and not ashamed to proclaim God in any situation, told us all to meet down at the pool and surround the pool and join hands.

One of the parts of the concert that we performed was a medley of songs, including the Bill Gather song 'Something About That Name.' During that song, one of the guys had an unbelievably moving speaking part. We all gathered around the pool, joined hands, and began singing. The college kids were taken by surprise and couldn't believe what they were seeing.

When it came time for Billy to do his speaking part, he climbed up the ladder to the high dive and did his part from up there. It seemed to echo off the motel's walls as though on a theater stage. By that time, there was complete silence. Most of us were moved to tears as we almost always were during that part of the concert. I don't remember exactly what happened after that, but there's no doubt that anyone who witnessed that moment never forgot it.

I don't remember all the places we visited while sharing this concert, but bits and pieces still stand out in my memory. That trip turned out to be one of the best times of my entire life up until that point. Even though it was terrifying for me in the beginning, I believe now that it was a monumental milestone for me as a young boy. It has made an everlasting impact on me.

Chapter III

Late Teens (Late 1970's)

By the time I was about sixteen years old, I had gone forward to church one Sunday and decided to dedicate my life to Christian ministry. Growing up and spending so much time at church, I had always heard guest speakers that came to share their testimony about how God had turned their life around and changed them from the inside out. At a young age, I was always moved by their stories. That's when I asked God to give me a story to tell, and as you will see, He did just that!

After the Florida trip in the summer of 1974, we continued to travel to various churches performing the Touch of the Holy Spirit concert and even going to the Nation's Capital, Washington DC, one summer. While taking a group tour through the Capitol, Benny, being the spontaneous personality that he was, had us all break out into the Halleluia Chorus right in the Capitol Rotunda while other people were taking tours. This was probably 1976, when the Country was celebrating the 200-year bi-centennial, and the capitol was crowded with people.

This was years before what we now know as a 'flash mob,' but everyone stopped in their tracks to listen just as they do today. Partly because they were shocked at what we were doing and also amazed at the acoustics in the capitol rotunda. I just knew that we were all going to be arrested, but we weren't, and it was a great experience, to say the least.

Many of the original members had now grown up and gone to college, while others just seemed to move on to other things. The group stayed together and continued to perform the concert for a while, even after Benny and Annette accepted another position at a church in Tennessee. A former minister of music at our church stepped in to keep the group together for a short time, but as with many good things, it eventually ended, and the group dissolved in 1977.

Once the group dissolved, I found myself without purpose. Church and this group had been my existence since early childhood and throughout my youth. All of my friends from church didn't live anywhere near us, and they all went to different schools other than where I went, so for the first time in my life, I felt lost.

Brad and I have been best friends since his family moved to the cul-de-sac where we grew up. Brad was also involved in the youth group, so we stayed pretty close even after the group split up. We spent most of our time fishing and hunting in our later teenage years, especially after getting our driver's licenses and becoming more independent.

High school for me was, let's just say, not a good experience. I didn't have many friends, and my grades were suffering, to say the least. The friends I did hang out with were not a good influence on me, and I started experimenting with skipping school and getting into trouble.

I had missed so many days in my eleventh-grade year that I had to retake that year. My parents were very displeased with the lifestyle I had chosen, and the new group of friends I was getting involved with, and they even considered sending me to military school. I swore up and down that, if they did, I would run away, and they would never see me again. I had no intention of actually running away and really didn't even know the extent of what I was even saying. It was just a tactical move on my part to try and see how serious they were.

Needless to say, I didn't get shipped off to military school, and I tried the eleventh grade again, but it was actually worse this time around because I was with a whole different group of people that were younger than I was and about halfway through my second round of eleventh grade, I quit school. I remember my dad telling me that if I wasn't going to go to school, I was going to go to work for him.

This was just another challenge for me. I mean, how hard could that be, working for your dad? I was the boss's son. No more having to get up early for school and work for Dad; this was going to be a breeze! The rude awakening came the very next morning when my brother-in-law burst through my bedroom door at 7:00 am, grabbed me by my ankles, and dragged me nearly out onto the floor. "I'm leaving in five minutes, and you better be ready and in the truck."

The telephone company that my brother-in-law worked for as his regular job was on strike, so he was filling in working for my dad. He was a stocky build with biceps bigger than my thighs and not one you wanted to mess with. Needless to say, I was up and, in the truck, maybe not within five minutes, but not a whole lot longer than that. It turned out my dad had plans for him to give me all of the grunt work, probably in hopes of scaring me into begging to go back to school, but that didn't turn out to be the case.

I loved the work. I was just young and stupid enough not to care at that point as long as I wasn't at school. My dad made sure I started at the very bottom. I wasn't given special privileges because I was the boss's son. In fact, it was just the opposite. He wanted to scare me more than anything and show me that work wasn't a breeze, but at the same time, he was teaching me much more about work ethic than he even knew at the time.

We jumped around from job site to job site doing various kinds of work, but the real work I was interested in doing was carpentry. I developed a love for the smell of wood at a very early age when my dad used to take me to work with him in the summer, and the early experience left me with an overwhelming desire to learn how they created things the way they did from just pieces of wood.

My Uncle Tom was an all-around gifted carpenter and craftsman and could make just about anything from scraps of lumber. I spent much of my childhood hanging out on the job sites with the guys, soaking up everything I could from them. They made everything they did look easy, and where they learned all that they knew, I'll never know. This was back in the early fifties and sixties when I was a very small kid hanging out and learning from them. They didn't have all of the fancy power tools that we do today, so it was truly a craftsman's art.

I eventually worked my way up to working on one of my brothers' crews. He had a business in Versailles, so I got to work with that crew framing houses. I loved every aspect of the trade, and while I was being groomed to someday take on the business, I just saw it as something exciting to do, and I loved working out in the sun in the summer and then having indoor work when winter arrived.

Chapter IV

1st Marriage (1977)

The cute little blonde girl that showed up on the family farm that day became a part of my entire childhood and youth growing up. While her family didn't attend the same church as us, she attended bible school there in the summer when we were younger, and then she joined the Conquerors soon after it started up, so we both spent a lot of time together off and on during our childhood and teenage years. We never really dated, but I guess you could say I had a crush on her from day one.

Our family lived in Lexington, and her family lived in Versailles, which was in the next county over from where I grew up, so the encounters were mostly church-related in our later teenage years until her family moved to Lexington during our junior or senior year of high school.

Her parents bought their first home from my dad. When they decided to move to Lexington, they contacted him again and eventually purchased another home from him, literally two minutes from where we lived. It wasn't until then that we actually started dating pretty seriously, and after graduation, we got married.

Chapter V

Building My Own Home (1977)

After Sissy and I got married, we picked out a lot in one of the subdivisions where my dad was building some houses in Versailles and applied for a loan to start construction on a house. The loan was approved, and we began work right away.

I had already been working in this same subdivision for a year, building the same style of homes we would be building for ourselves. However, this was the first one I would attempt to build on my own without the supervision of another foreman. Dad would monitor our progress on a daily basis and answer any questions I had regarding the framing, which was the most crucial part of the construction.

There were many questions and trips to some of the previous homes we had recently framed in the subdivision to compare measurements and ensure I didn't screw something up. This was a big challenge and a learning experience that would be the foundation for many more houses over the years.

Me and Letcher, a guy from one of the other crews, did most of the work that we could do until we got to the point where we needed some extra pairs of hands to get the roof on and get it dried in, so dad recruited some of his workers from another job site to come and help. Once we got it dried in, we went back to just me and Letcher. Letcher had worked on the crew a little longer than I had, so he had a little more experience, but he could not be left in charge of getting the job done.

It took us a lot longer than it should have, but then again, there were only two of us, and neither of us was a seasoned carpenter, so we just kept going and eventually finished it. It was definitely a learning experience, but for me, it seemed very natural, and I loved doing every aspect of the process. I stayed on the job site all day, even after regular working hours putting in the extra touch to make it my own.

It was more than just a house to me. More than just an accomplishment that I had completed. It was personal. Something that I had created from the ground up with my own two hands, and I was very proud of that little house at the end of the cul-de-sac. Yes, ironically enough as it seems, I had lived my whole childhood on a cul-de-sac, and now I was building a future at another location in one as well.

Sissy helped with some of the construction along the way because she wasn't just a pretty blonde-haired girl; she had quite the tomboy streak and wasn't afraid of getting her hands dirty. She picked out the colors for the exterior brick, roof, shutters, and interior finishes. It was a joint effort, to say the least, and when it was all said and done, it was perfect.

Chapter VI

Fall From Grace (1978)

After the house was complete and we were getting settled into the new life we had begun, we were still attending the same church and doing life pretty much the same, except we were now married and out on our own.

We were living our best life, invincible and indestructible, or so we thought. We didn't worry about stuff back then; we just lived life every day. We weren't angels by any stretch of the imagination, but back then, we didn't have all the distractions associated with teenagers and young adults today. It was just life and a good one at that.

Even though life was treating us well, we were both adventurous and sometimes a little promiscuous, which eventually led us apart and headed in two different directions with our lives. I spent a lot more of my free time hanging out with the boys fishing and being away from home, and she was drawn back to some of her old friends from school there in Versailles, and we soon began to go in separate directions.

With a divorce hanging over my head, my pastor took me to lunch one day and told me that if I went through with the divorce, I would never be able to hold a position in the church. The decision wasn't mine alone to make, and the divorce was most likely taking place, so for the church to turn its back on me was devastating news. After all, I had made the commitment to dedicate my life to full-time ministry, and now that option was no longer on the table.

This was the 1970s, and back then, the church was probably a little stricter than they are today on divorce, but at the time, that was how it was, and I knew that my future had just been turned upside down. I felt called to work in the youth ministry, and I didn't understand why the church was turning its back on me. It seemed as if the only people that I knew to turn to for help were the very ones turning their back on me. If this was how the church would treat me, then I didn't want any part of it. I decided I was going to start doing life my way.

As part of the divorce agreement, I ended up buying out my half of the house, which I didn't want to part with because I had a personal attachment to it and wasn't about to let it go. After the dust settled, I was a single twenty-year-old with his own house.

My childhood friend Brad moved in with me to help share some of the costs of home ownership, and it didn't take long for us to figure out how to get our hands on some beer and start inviting some friends over. The party life had never really been for me, mostly because I was always the shy type, and I wasn't even old enough to purchase alcohol. But, as the old saying goes, "Where there's a will, there's a way," and it didn't take long for us to figure out a way.

When you're a young single guy who owns his own house, new friends start showing up everywhere. I don't even remember where they came from because I didn't really know a lot of people there in Versailles. It started with just a few of our friends from Lexington, and it didn't take long for the word to get out, and the party was on!

Before I knew it, it was party after party. As I said, I was a shy kid and didn't have many friends outside of the church, so the popularity of being the guy with the party pad grew on me quickly. The drinking wasn't a problem for me at this point. In fact, it was only the beginning of the party lifestyle, and mainly just on the weekends, but looking back, I can see that this decision was the beginning of what would eventually end up being the point of no return.

Chapter VII

2nd Marriage (1980)

I was still working for my dad, and by this time, I was working in a subdivision in Mt. Sterling, Kentucky which was an hour's drive for me from Versailles. Brad was still living with me at the house and worked with me, so we rode to work together.

It wasn't anything for us to party all night and then drive all the way to work the next day, work a solid day, and drive back home. In fact, that's the first time that I remember getting involved with smoking weed. We would roll a couple of joints in the morning, smoke one on the way to work, and then smoke another on the way home.

Back then, weed wasn't like it is today. We smoked a lot of Mexican weed full of seeds and shake. Every now and then, we would come across some good buds, but for the most part, it was crap, but we smoked it nonetheless.

During one of our usual weekend parties, I happened to notice an unfamiliar face in the crowd. A red-haired girl, but not your average ginger with pale skin. More like a strawberry blonde with a tanned skin tone. The alcohol made me a lot more confident than my normal sober shy self, and I was quick to strike up a conversation with her.

Her name was Laurie, and we started dating soon after that, and we eventually got married in November of 1979. After a couple of years of marriage, our son, James Thomas, was born in September

1982. Named after my father, James, the name Thomas came from my name and Laurie's dad's middle name. He had the same strawberry blonde hair and skin tone as his mother. My first-born son. Someone to carry on the Carr name.

This was when I started up my photography business there in Versailles. I had always had a love for photography, and up until this point, it was just a hobby, with an occasional wedding or two. I had rented a space in downtown Versailles for my studio, but I didn't have enough business to sustain the rent on such a large space, so I had to come up with a different option.

Laurie worked for a chiropractor there in Versailles, and he rented an office space from my dad but didn't need the whole space, so I rented the front half of the second unit to use as a studio. It was right on the main road leading into Versailles, and I was finally starting to get a clientele built up. Life was good, and I was living the dream.

I was also a local Jaycees (Junior Chamber of Commerce) member and was pretty involved in the community. The Jaycees would hold various events throughout the year, like our fall festival, golf events, and Christmas tree sales raising money for our annual kids' Christmas event that we held every year for the less fortunate children in our community.

The Christmas event was an awesome time. We would go to our local toy store there in Versailles after hours and use the lists that were provided to us by the parents of the kids, and we would shop and purchase everything on the kid's lists. Then, at our annual Christmas event, Santa, whom my dad played the part of for several years, would call out the kids' names and pass out their presents. The looks on the kids' faces were priceless. They had the best time ever! Those were some good times making many great memories and lifelong friends, but like all good things; it would come to an end.

Chapter VIII

Divorce #2 (Addiction Building)

During this time, the partying continued, and now with so many more friends from the Versailles area, we were having a lot of parties at our house and mostly drinking with the occasional party extras on the side like a little weed and speed. I made many new friends from being involved in the community and having a second part-time photography business, and life seemed good.

Laurie and I still attended church fairly regularly as a family, but our lifestyle wasn't Godly, and our marriage suffered because of it. Eventually, we separated and divorced after about seven years of marriage. I also ended up with the house after this divorce because it was mine before we married. At the time, I had the steadiest income and place to live, so I was trying to gain custody of Jamie.

He was staying with Laurie's parents during the separation because neither of us was budging on custody, and their home was the more stable place for him at the time. I don't remember how long the separation went on, but I do know that my chances of gaining joint custody were looking pretty good for me at that time.

Unfortunately, the consequences of my actions over the coming months would prove to be damaging for me as far as custody went. Eventually, all parties agreed that the more stable place for Jamie would be with Laurie's parents until one or the other of us could provide a stable environment for him.

Neither of us was ready to be single parents. Even though I was hoping to try and gain joint custody, I was single again and not emotionally in a place where I was ready to take that on, no matter how hard I tried to be strong and prove that I was.

This separation and divorce had left me a very hard-hearted and bitter man, and though I could not see it then, this is what I would later realize as the early stages of depression. I thought I was being strong on the outside, but inside, I wasn't ready for my life to be turned upside down, and the divorce was hard on me emotionally.

My way of battling the depression and the feeling of helplessness was pushing it under the rug and ignoring it. The only time that I felt like myself was when I was drinking or high. By this time, I was experimenting with whatever I could get my hands on that gave me a buzz and took my mind off reality.

Anything from weed to mushrooms to ecstasy to LSD to speed to Xanax. Whatever it took. I didn't care about the consequences; I was just trying to survive my way. The sheltered life I had grown up with was for my own good, but now that I was experiencing life in the fast lane, I was making up for lost ground. I was young and stupid and didn't really give it a second thought.

Joey was a friend of mine whom I had met through one of Laurie's cousins, and he had moved in with me as a roommate around the same time. He had a good job working in Lexington at a food distribution company, and the rent he was paying helped me keep up with the mortgage and utilities. We became close friends despite our age difference, and he liked to party just as much as I did.

One day while working in Lexington, we had gotten rained out, so we stopped by a nightclub in Lexington to have a couple of drinks in the middle of the day. There was nobody there except for the owner and the manager. During our conversation, they mentioned they were looking for someone to build a deck at the back of the nightclub. This was right up our alley, so to speak, and we began talking about giving him a bid for the job.

As stupid as we were back then, we accepted the job, and in return for our labor, we would be given an unlimited supply of drinks and admission to the bar. It wasn't a contract or anything, more like a mutual agreement. I mean, we really needed money, but the offer was too good to refuse for either of us, and we agreed to do the work. That would have been the spring and summer of 1986.

Rick and I had been working together for a while on various construction jobs. He was Laurie's cousin, and he and I had become good friends while Laurie and I were married. We enjoyed working together on some construction jobs, and we liked to party, so this was going to be an adventure, to say the least. We started work on the deck almost immediately. We gave them a list of materials, and they were delivered within a few days, so we recruited a few other guys to help and get started.

We would work on the deck all day, go home, get cleaned up, change clothes and head back to the club for a night of partying. The more work we would do on the deck, the more they would add to it, and before it was over, we had created a whole new outdoor area for the nightclub. It was nice. We had an unlimited budget to work with, and the owner loved our recommendations for seating around the walls and an outdoor bar area.

We worked on that project throughout the summer. I was going through the same routine nearly every day. Working and drinking all day, then partying and drinking all night. One night, the manager asked me to give his niece a ride home on my way to Versailles. They lived in Georgetown, so it wasn't really that far out of the way for me, and besides, he was good to us, so I agreed to give her a ride.

I really never should have agreed, and to be honest, he should never have asked, given the condition that I was in. I had been working in the sun all day, all the while we were drinking most of the day as well, but it was just another day like any other since we had been there working on the deck, so he didn't think anything of it, and neither did I at the time.

I don't even remember leaving the nightclub that night. I have moments from that night that I remember during the drive, like nodding off and waking up, but for the most part, it was all blank. Needless to say, I didn't drop her off at her house because she was still in the truck when I fell asleep at the wheel and wrecked the truck.

I was so intoxicated that I still don't remember the wreck at all. I had run off the shoulder of the road just a few miles from my house and rolled the truck three times. I was ejected from the truck at approximately sixty miles an hour, according to the police report, and his niece was trapped in the truck and had sustained multiple injuries, including a broken leg.

I vaguely remember waking up in the hospital while they were trying to get X-rays of my back. I had multiple cuts and bruises all over my body, and it was later determined that I had crushed two of the vertebrae in my back. We were both very lucky to be alive.

To try and help jar any memory I might have of the wreck, I went down to the site where it happened and it was very surreal. There was about a quarter mile of wooden cattle fence that was taken out. You could see the tracks where I veered off the road and into the ditch line, eventually spinning and rolling the truck down the fence line. You would think this would have been a wake-up call for me, but it didn't faze me. In fact, I was right back at the nightclub the very next night, drinking again.

The weekend parties consisted of drinking and smoking weed and a little speed and blotter acid, also known as LSD, a hallucinogenic drug. You talk about wild and crazy stuff; that is no comparison to the mildly manageable buzz from smoking a little weed. I saw pictures melt and run down the wall. Couches and furniture breathing. It's crazy what your mind can convince you of while under the influence. As scary as some of it was, I couldn't wait to get more and do it again.

It wasn't something I would have ever done by myself, however. We only dropped acid when there were several of us together on the weekend, and we never left the house. Well, except for one night. We decided to go for a little drive in the country, but I don't think we managed to get off our street before one of us fell out of the car. I don't even think we made it out of the driveway; that's how crazy this stuff is.

Needless to say, none of this behavior was helping my relationship with my son. I had chosen a lifestyle I knew wasn't appropriate for a child to be around, and in the back of my mind, I knew I was making stupid decisions. But on the surface, I was fine as far as anyone else knew. Still, the battle that was going on in my head was deafening. The demons had set up shop in my head, and the only thing that seemed to keep them quiet was the drugs.

I still made an attempt to spend as much time with Jamie as I could when I was sober, but at the same time, I was indulging in even more behavior that wasn't healthy for a young child to be around, and he was in a more stable environment, so I was okay with leaving well enough alone. I don't think Jamie had a clue what I was involved in. He just wanted to spend time with his dad, and I was so consumed with my lifestyle that I failed him and let him down more than I even knew at the time.

Even though I managed to carry myself well on the surface and even continued regularly working inside, I was dying a little more each day. The battle in my mind wouldn't allow me to see clearly enough to discern right from wrong emotionally. I never once returned to the God I knew as a child for help. I thought He had abandoned me or at least didn't want anything to do with me because of the person I had become.

I was young enough that even with the self-destructive abuse I was putting my body through, I could still carry on and function daily. All while keeping that veil that separated my inner demons from reality pulled tightly enough that it was not to be exposed to anyone around me.

My parents and family didn't have a clue how serious any of this was at the time. I'm sure they knew I wasn't living the lifestyle that they had hoped for me as an adult, but they never confronted me with the reality of my situation if they knew. I guess I was just good at hiding it. After all, I was showing up for work every day and even managing side jobs at the same time. Everything on the outside appeared to be fine, while on the inside, I knew that this wasn't the life I was designed to live, but I just didn't know how to get there or if I could.

Chapter IX

The Truth Is Revealed

A few days after Joey and I were arrested in April of 1987, as mentioned at the beginning of this journey, my parents were back from their little getaway, so I called them to tell them what had happened, and they came and bailed me out of jail and took me to their house to stay. I was still in shock from the arrest and the last few days I had spent in that jail, so I was fine staying at their house for a few days.

My parents were confused about how I could have gotten so mixed up with these people and why their baby was treated so wrong. Someone else must be at fault. This was not how they had raised me, and even though I believe my dad had a pretty good idea that I wasn't the innocent baby that my mom insisted I was, he never really confronted me about any of it.

I don't think that they understood any of it. They were just good, hard-working, all-around decent people who had never been involved in anything like this. None of my siblings had ever been in any kind of trouble with the law either, but leave it to me to be the one to change all that.

After a few days to calm down, my dad drove me to my house to get a few clothes and check on my house. If you remember, they confiscated my truck, so I had no transportation. When the detectives were questioning us, they told me that I would never see that truck again and that they would turn my house inside out, looking for any evidence of my involvement with Joey. I really think that they believed I was Joey's main connection for the cocaine and that I was delivering it to him the night they arrested the two of us.

I was afraid to even go into my house. A mutual friend had been staying at the house for a few days during that same time, so I assumed he would have been around if the detectives came with a search warrant, but he wasn't anywhere to be found when I went there that day. The house hadn't been touched, so I assumed then that they were bluffing when they told me they would tear it apart.

Nevertheless, I still thought they were watching my every move, and for all I knew, they may have even placed listening devices throughout the house. I wasn't about to stay there that night. I just wanted to get in, get a few clothes, ensure no incriminating evidence was around, and get out. At the time, I hadn't started putting the pieces of the puzzle together, but I would eventually start putting the missing pieces together, and the truth would reveal itself.

Nobody was around, not even the girl I was dating at the time. I figured it was because they were all aware of our arrest and were staying clear of Joey and me for fear of being watched.

The girl I was dating at the time had shown up at our front door one day while I was at work, but Joey happened to be at home. She was selling Kirby vacuum cleaners. He told her that I was working and she could return later and talk to me, which she actually did, and not only did she talk me into a vacuum cleaner, I talked her into a date.

I don't know any of this encounter to be factual, but the more I processed the events leading up to our arrest, the more sense it was beginning to make. Nancy had shown up at the house posing as a vacuum cleaner salesperson, began to hang out with us on a pretty regular basis, and knew our every move. The day of our arrest, I hadn't heard anything from her. I just assumed she was working out of town that day.

The mysterious part for me was that she didn't show up or call after that day. As far as I know, nobody had talked with her and told her what was going on, so how would she know to stay away? I'm no detective, but I have that instinctive curiosity that keeps me searching for answers, and things weren't adding up. She was looking more and more like an informant to me.

When it came time to start the court process, I wasn't settling for a court-appointed attorney. Joey had hired an attorney, so I started searching for one because our cases were being tried separately. I found a criminal defense attorney that came highly recommended by a family member, but when I gave him a call, he told me $10,000 with half up front. I think I was able to talk him down on the amount, but it was still a lot of money for me.

The only way I was going to be able to afford that was to get a line of credit toward the equity of the house. I was confident that this guy would get me off without any jail time. I was facing 10-15 years for trafficking in a controlled substance, but they didn't find anything on me when they arrested us because Joey had it in his pocket, so I was pretty confident that a good lawyer could get me out of it, or at least get the charges reduced to a misdemeanor or something a little more realistic.

After several months of the court process, a plea agreement was reached to reduce the charges to possessing a controlled substance. I agreed to a five-year probation and served six months in the county jail on work release. I wasn't happy with the plea agreement, especially since I didn't possess the cocaine. It was, however, found in my truck, so I was ultimately responsible.

I agreed to the plea agreement on one condition that they would release my truck back to me because it was my only source of transportation, and I needed it for work. They were reluctant to agree, but I pressed my attorney to get it back for me and earn some of that nearly ten grand I forked out for his services.

I can remember smoking part of a joint on the way to pick up Joey from work that night, and I had laid what was left of it in the ashtray when I got to his work. I just knew that they had found that when they searched the vehicle, but when the truck was returned to me, low and behold, there was that joint still laying in the ashtray as it had been the entire time it was on the impound lot. Needless to say, I enjoyed the rest of it on the way home that day.

Chapter X

3rd Marriage (1988)

While serving my six months jail sentence and on work release, it wasn't just working all day, then back to jail. In fact, I was almost never going to work. Dad would pick me up from jail in the morning; I would grab breakfast at my parent's house, then head to Versailles to spend the day hanging out with friends down at the river, drinking and partying.

I spent way too much time jeopardizing my work release agreement and, in reality, putting my dad in a position where he could get in much trouble because he wasn't supervising me at all times like he was supposed to be according to his agreement with the work release program. All I wanted was out of jail for the day, and the consequences didn't matter to me. It was all about me, as it had been for most of my life.

The worst part about being out on work release each day was getting strip searched every night when I returned to the jail. That's one hundred and eighty strip searches. I would make fun of the guards because this was their job. Every single inmate returning from work release had to be strip searched every day. I found humor in the little things. I had to keep from going insane.

I actually did manage to do a little work while out on work release. In fact, I was working on a house in Lexington for my dad, doing some trim carpentry, and when I arrived at the job site one day, I recognized the bricklayer as James. He was one of Dad's bricklayers from Powell County whom my dad had used for years. He was laying the brick on the house where I was working. I had known James and his family for a long time while working in Mt. Sterling all those years.

James had a bunch of children, ten altogether, and he worked a lot of them on the various job sites, and I knew most of them except for this one that was helping him with this house. I thought it must be his granddaughter or something because she looked so much younger than all the other kids I knew.

It turned out it wasn't his granddaughter at all. It was his daughter, Nita. She was one of the two youngest daughters and still in school back when James was bricking houses for my dad in Mt. Sterling, and that's why I never really knew her or her younger sister.

I was impressed with how she could manhandle a five-gallon bucket full of mortar, one in each hand, and hand them up the scaffold one section above her. I had done that type of work before, and I knew it wasn't an easy task, even for a guy, but for a small girl of her stature, she was handling it pretty well.

I saw her on the job nearly every weekday while they were bricking the house. I knew that the job would soon come to an end, and they would be pulling out soon, so if I were going to make a move, it would have to be soon. So, as fate would have it, I asked for her number so we could keep in touch, and we eventually hooked up one weekend (while I was supposed to be out on work release), and a relationship soon began.

I finished serving my six months sentence, and Nita eventually moved in with me, and we began working together on various construction jobs. It wasn't common back then to see a woman working on a construction site, but she could hold her own with just about any of the guys.

By the time I had finished serving my jail time, the nightclub days had fizzled out, and things weren't the same there anymore. Many of the people we knew and partied with had all moved on, and I just didn't have much interest in going there anymore. I lost touch with Joey after Nita, and I got together. He had moved back in with his parents after we were arrested, and we both went in different directions.

Nita and I married in the summer of 1988, and we kept working together for several years. She had a son named Brian from her previous marriage. He was three when we married and had been staying with Nita's mom while we dated, but after we got married, he moved in with us at the house there in Versailles.

Our daughter, Kelli Marie, was born in October 1991. Jamie was nine and still living with Laurie's parents by this time. I would have loved to take Jamie in as part of our family, but he was well cared for there, and I didn't want to screw it up for him by disrupting his life all over again, so I just tried to spend as much time with him and include him as much as possible.

Over the years of my marriage to Nita, weekends were filled with bonfires and camping at her family's place there in Eastern Kentucky. Times seemed to be good. At least we were having fun, and over the next several years, it was a pretty natural way of life for us. Nita had taken on a steadier job at a factory in Versailles, and I was still working on various construction jobs along the way.

Some of my favorite memories from that time period were hanging out with my brother-in-law, Jackie, and his wife, Rosie, at their house in Clay City, Kentucky. We were at their house nearly every weekend. The girls would hang out while the kids played, and we guys would tinker around in Jackie's shop or go fishing. It seemed like we were always working on something together.

It was just under an hour's drive from our house to theirs, but we didn't think anything of it when the weekend came, or a Kentucky basketball game was on. We just packed up the kids and took off.

There was always a house full of people for every Kentucky basketball game. Family and friends would always gather at their house to watch the game on their big screen TV. Not every household had a big-screen TV back then, so it was the place to be. Those were some good times. So much fun that I hated it when it was time to pack up the kids and head back home.

I felt at home there. Not that I didn't have a loving home and a family of my own, but it was fun, and we had some good times, and I needed that. I was starting to feel like I fit in somewhere. I had ruined so much of my life and walked away from the life I had hoped for as a youth that everything about this new life seemed to fit me.

At their house is where I first met Owl. He was one of Jackie's friends that lived there in Clay City. Just an old geezer that liked to pick on me and give me a hard time. They all did, but to me, it was fitting in. Everyone in Clay City and nearby Stanton seemed to have a nickname like Dribble, Diaper, or Cheesy, so it was only fitting when they settled on a nickname for me; Bait. That was the short version, and I will just leave it at that so I don't step on anyone's feelings.

Jackie used to introduce me to everyone as his gay brother-in-law from Versailles. Mind you, I was as straight as an arrow, but they thought it was humorous and got a kick out of it. Owl was the one that tagged me with the nickname, and it stuck like glue. It was a time when everyone joked around and played jokes on everyone else, so for them to include me, I felt right at home. No one got offended back then; it was just how it was, and life was good.

Owl was one of those guys that always seemed to be around or not very far away. He seemed a little older, but I think it was mostly because of the health issues that just made him look older. He had been through prostate cancer, and when they did the surgery, they found that cancer had spread to his colon and bladder, and they removed all of that. He spent the rest of his life dealing with a catheter and a colostomy bag. I guess that's better than the alternative.

One of the things I liked most about Jackie at first was his ability to grow some of the best weed I had ever smoked. I mean, premium stuff back then. He was a hardworking man that supported his family with a nice career in commercial construction, but his side hustle was a craft. That man knew how to do it, and I admired that about him.

We were always doing something together on the weekends, which was one reason why I liked to hang out with him so much. That and the fact that he always had some good pills. It was more of a casual thing for us back then; I guess you could say. It's not like we stayed smashed out of our minds all the time. It was more like a recreational thing we did while tinkering around in the shop or fishing.

This wasn't my first experience with pills, though. Over the years, I had experimented with a variety of different pills, but I had never really tried pain pills before. This was a new buzz and not one that left you paralyzed and unable to function. These were mild pain relievers compared to the pain medications today. I could actually function and go to work every day, but eventually, I had to have them go to work.

I didn't think I needed the weed and pills to manage life; I thought it was just recreational. At least, it seemed that way at the time. In reality, I needed all of it. I needed that friendship. I needed the buzz. I needed anything that made me feel happy because, in my head, that was the answer to everything. I couldn't just be happy without all of the self-medicating.

I didn't know what happiness was anymore. I remembered happier times without the supplemental aid of something other than life itself, but that was when I was so much younger, and life was easier then. What I failed to realize was that the battle was in my head the entire time. The hardest battle you will ever face is within your own head.

Chapter XI

Separation

The struggle within my head to find some sort of peace that I had sought for so long now had changed me in so many ways. The more I fought that battle in my mind, the stronger the demons attacked. There were days when I was on top of the world, happy, and then there were days when I found myself in the darkest of places.

If I just had a little more weed. If I just had a few more of those pills. Every waking hour of the day was becoming more and more of a struggle. The demons in my head told me; once you get a few more pills or a little weed, you'll feel a lot better and be able to do whatever you need. In reality, that was a lie.

I had lost all sense of reality around me. I was so deep in battle with the demons in my head that I couldn't even see I had everything I had ever wanted right before me. My family, home, friends, and the ability to earn money using the skills I had learned over the years. When I looked in the mirror, all I could see was failure after failure.

My marriage and family life were struggling because of the battles I was fighting in my head. None of that even seemed to matter to me anymore. I was just going through the motions of life, putting everyone and everything that mattered most behind me. I mean, I loved my family, but I wasn't putting them first, and I couldn't look past my self-pity to recognize that they were also suffering.

Nita eventually grew weary from the battles I was fighting within and asked for a divorce. I couldn't believe it. A third marriage was on the verge of ending, and I wasn't in any way prepared to handle that emotionally. I begged her not to leave me. I promised to turn over a new leaf and get my life back. I was making promises that I had no idea how to keep. I knew deep down that there was a better man inside of me somewhere; I just couldn't find him anymore.

I didn't try to change anything. I wasn't capable of changing anything. Instead of working to better myself, all I did was fall deeper into depression. I didn't even know that I was depressed; in fact, I don't know if anyone actually knows they are depressed; it's the state of mind that you're in. The battle within your head that tells you that you are fine, you just need to do some things a little differently to convince yourself everything will be all right, but at the same time, you also know it's not going to be all right.

Reality finally set in when I sat and watched her pack her things and load them into her car. Part of me wanted to fight back and try to keep her from taking anything at all, and part of me said it wouldn't last long; she would come running back to me after a week or two. That's how convinced I was that material possession like a nice house would make her want to stay, but it didn't.

The hardest thing about her leaving was watching her take the kids. That devastated me inside. First, it was Jamie's life that was turned upside down due to my selfish ignorance; now, it is happening again with Brian and Kelli. Brian wasn't my son, but I had been a part of his life for so long that it still hurt to see him go. I couldn't see what I was doing wrong. I was just trying to cope each day, but the steps I was taking to make things better in my mind only made them worse for the people I loved.

Chapter XII

Divorce #3

I found myself alone again in an empty house. It had survived three marriages and more memories than I could count. Nearly twenty years had passed since I had built that house. Everything there reminded me of happier times. That didn't seem to help at all; in fact, it only made matters a lot worse. Everywhere I looked, there were memories. How could I be in this position? I mean, I had so much potential going for me at one point in my life, and now I sit in an empty house all alone. I had to do something quickly, or I would lose it all.

I had signed up for a mail-in home inspection course a few months earlier, and as part of that course, it not only taught you about the home inspection process, but it also came with a computer. At least, that's what the ad said. Yes, it came with a computer, but I had to build it myself as part of the course. Once I completed each step of the course, I would mail in my answer book, and they would mail me a new set of books and some more computer parts.

Remember that this was before the internet, so online courses weren't a thing yet. Everything was still done through the mail. The course I was taking would eventually teach me the process of home inspections which was still in its very early stages of existence. With my experience in construction, I felt like this would be a perfect fit for my future. Could this finally be the answer to a more successful future? Perhaps, but I still needed money to keep up with the responsibilities of owning a home.

At some point during my last marriage, I remembered that we consolidated some bills and applied them toward our mortgage. Among that consolidation was the line of credit I had taken out to pay for my attorney years before. I assumed that when they consolidated the payments, they had closed that line of credit, but in fact, all they did was pay it off, and the actual line of credit still existed.

This was huge for me. I was back in business again. A $10,000 line of credit was the answer to everything. I could catch up on some bills and still manage to keep the house. Money has a way of making anyone feel good, right? At least, it did for me at that time. I had to hide it from Nita, though. If she found out, she would be entitled to half of it if the divorce went through, and that wouldn't happen.

With the home inspection course now completed and the computer all built, all that was left to do was start up a new business and get in on the ground floor of this new home inspection gig. That proved not to be as easy as it sounded, however. All it did for me at the time was equip me with the knowledge of home inspections and get me a computer. The computer was useless to me other than a way to play a few games I found on floppy discs at Radio Shack.

I used some of the money from the line of credit to purchase a better computer from the store equipped with all the necessary software to run programs. The thing that I learned from the course was how to build a computer from the ground up, which is still helpful for me today. With my knowledge of the inner workings of the computer, I know how to install and upgrade the basic hardware, and I know my way around the basic structure of the computer.

Once I got the upgraded computer, I started working with spreadsheets and Word documents. I had done some experimenting with writing some poems early on in my teenage years using a typewriter, but this computer took it to a whole new level. I had always enjoyed math in school, so the spreadsheets were a fun learning experience for me, and I began to develop a spreadsheet that could help me calculate construction bids.

Looking back, that was huge for me. I never did graduate high school, and society considered me a dropout incapable of making anything of my life. I didn't need a piece of paper to tell me I was worthy. I was, and still am, an entrepreneur of sorts. I create ways to earn money based on my skill level. The computer would one day prove to be a huge asset for me when it came to earning an income and supporting myself.

Chapter XIII

All The Wrong Places

It was maybe a year after our separation that the divorce was final, and the time to move on was now. By this time, it was around 1995, and things weren't the best, but I managed to keep the house and earn a little money here and there, picking up side jobs.

I had found new possibilities through the internet, which was becoming a household name by then. I can remember logging on to the internet for the first time. I received a CD in the mail from AOL (America Online), and this was revolutionary. It was through the telephone lines and was called a dial-up connection. I can still hear the sound it made while logging on. The possibilities would be endless with all the new options made available by the World Wide Web, and I was ready to explore it all.

This was about the same time I started taking an interest in graphic design. I had always thought that it would be cool to be able to incorporate graphics into my photography. After all, I remember when I was much younger, I would take pictures of my niece with my dad's Polaroid camera and write descriptions in the little white space below the photo. That was graphic design, 1970s style.

I learned of a new computer software called Adobe Photoshop through the internet. It could do everything I had imagined with photos and much more. I purchased a copy of the program and began to teach myself how to use it. It was great for photo restoration and even great for adding graphics to images. Needless to say, I was hooked right from the start, and this would prove to be the beginning of a new era for me. One that I still use on a daily basis.

When I wrecked my truck several years before, it left me with two collapsed vertebrae and chronic pain in my back, so I didn't pursue any heavier construction jobs. I mostly spent my time in front of the computer learning all I could and experimenting with various techniques. The internet made it possible for me to research new possibilities. With my entrepreneurial instincts, the new ideas would eventually consume me, and I found myself sitting at the computer for hours on end, learning everything I could.

Even through the separation and divorce, I maintained my relationship with my daughter, Kelli. I tried to go and pick her up for the weekend every chance I could. I knew she loved coming to spend time with me, and this was my reason for living. I couldn't bring myself to let her down. In her eyes, I was everything. She had no way of knowing everything that was going on with me emotionally because I kept that buried deep within me. When Kelli and I were together, I tried to just have fun with her. She was still very young, and grownup stuff didn't mean anything to her.

I would say that I spent the next couple of years going through the motions of life. I was spending way too much time on the internet, and work had become minimal, to say the least. I had purchased a nice printer with some of the money left in the equity line of credit and was making tickets for bands performing around where I lived in Versailles. The graphics work was mostly making fliers, posters, and tickets for these bands, but all I was getting out of it was the experience.

I just wanted to build up the name and get the stuff out there in front of the public, hoping it would someday take off and the business would grow. That didn't really ever happen, though. The expense of keeping the house and all of the bills quickly caught up with me, and the bank account was getting lower and lower with each passing day.

During this time, a friend of mine there in Versailles introduced me to the newest craze in pain medication called OxyContin. I remember that day like it was yesterday. Before that, the most powerful pills we got were Percocet and Lortab and the occasional methadone when all else failed. He had a prescription for them because of his chronic back pain due to a work-related injury. He was on workman's comp disability and would often stop by and hang out with me during the day.

We proceeded to peel the outer skin from the pills and then crush them up and snort them. They were supposed to be time-released, but it sure didn't take any time for it to hit me like a ton of bricks. Out of nowhere, I started sweating profusely, and I knew what was coming. I had to get some fresh air, but as soon as I stepped out onto the back patio, I started dry heaving. Apparently, you shouldn't take pain medication on an empty stomach, and I had never experienced anything that powerful before.

That should have been a sign for me to stay away from those, but just as with any other drug I had experimented with in the past, that wasn't going to stop me. Once I recovered from that episode, I had to have more. As with any drug, the first time is always the best. You spend the rest of your time trying to chase the euphoria of that initial buzz, but as illusional as that is, you convince yourself that maybe, just maybe, the next one will get you back there.

When the pain pills or methadone weren't available, and I was just sick from the withdrawals, I would go to the emergency room at a hospital in Lexington to see if I could get any relief. It worked for the first few times, but all I ever got was a few mild hydrocodone, but they eventually caught on to what I was doing, and after several attempts, they would just put me in a back room until I got tired of waiting and I just walked out.

Months passed, and by this time, I had convinced myself that I needed to file for disability. All I needed was a good doctor to sign off on my previous back injury and a good lawyer to process the necessary papers. I could get approved for disability and not only get a nice check each month but also a monthly supply of pain pills. I mean, I knew so many people that had been successful, and I figured, why not give it a try?

I managed to go through the process of filing for the disability, but finding a good doctor at that time to sign off on my condition proved harder than I originally thought. I went all the way through the process, and they eventually denied my claim. I could have fought it, but I just didn't have it in me to continue fighting a losing battle and eventually gave up on the idea of that farfetched dream.

Chapter XIV

Foreclosure

I managed to keep it going for a while, but the upkeep on the house was lacking at this point. After nearly twenty years, things started getting old, and breakdowns were common as far as the plumbing and general upkeep. I managed to make as minimal repairs as possible, just enough to make it by, but it was never the same as it once was. I couldn't believe that I had let my house get into the neglected shape it was in.

I'm sure my neighbors were aware that something was wrong because I had always kept things so neat and manicured, and that definitely wasn't the case anymore, especially with the yard. I rarely even mowed the grass anymore, which was not my style at all. I was always so proud of my home, and how I kept it up showed.

I kept getting letters in the mail from my mortgage company about the delinquent account, but I just ignored them and tried to put that out of my mind. Mostly because I knew that there wasn't any way I could catch up on my payments, and asking my family for help was out of the question because I didn't want to burden them any more than I already had so many times before. I guess I was just holding out hope for a miracle or something.

In 1998, almost twenty years from the day the house was completed, the sheriff served me papers that I had thirty days to make the account current or the bank would sue for foreclosure. If that happened, they would force me out and set a date to auction the property. Even though I knew this was reality and would soon lose my home, I wouldn't allow that to sink in. I think it was due to the advanced stage of my depression. I refused to accept reality, even though in the back of my mind, I knew it would happen very soon.

Once the thirty days had passed, the court date was set for the foreclosure process. I didn't even show up for court when the date rolled around. They set a date for the auction on the courthouse steps. I wasn't about to show up for that! You talk about humiliation. After once being nominated for president of the Jaycees to being forced out of my home at a public auction.

Once the auction had taken place and everything was finalized, they gave me thirty days to vacate the property. I hadn't even packed up any of my belongings. I didn't want to accept that I would lose my home. I had already sold off many items of any value just to keep the power on, so there wasn't much of anything to pack up with any value other than a few personal items.

My sister Jackie came down with one of Dad's trucks and helped me pack up what little was left. I didn't want either of my parents to be there. It was bad enough having to walk away from all the memories. I don't even know how I managed to keep from falling apart. I guess I blocked it out because I was leaving behind so much of my life, so many memories that those walls held inside. I still carry many of those memories with me today.

Occasionally, I will drive by that house when I am in the area, and I can still see a much younger me walking the top of the walls setting trusses, laying down the roof sheathing and mowing the grass, or working on something. For the most part, the house still looks much like it did back then, except the trees are much bigger, and they now have a fence around the front yard. So much has changed in my life since that house, but a part of me will always remember the many good times it holds.

Chapter XV

Depression Sets In

Once I moved out of my house, the only place that I had to go was my parents' house. The same house that I grew up in. My mom was so excited for me to be coming back home. She had it in her mind that I would be moving back into my old room upstairs across the hall from their room, just like it was back in the day. I had different plans, though, and they didn't include my old room.

There was no way that I could move back into my old room after being gone for twenty years. Of course, it was the best place for me because it had a nice bed with clean sheets and a television, with a bathroom right next door. I didn't want any of that. I didn't even want to be there at all, but I had nowhere else to go, so I had to make something I could call my own.

Against my mom's wishes, I told her I would be making a place in the basement. What could be so bad about that? Many people live in their basements and have nice accommodations, but this basement wasn't your average. It wasn't even finished. It still had the exposed floor joists above and concrete block walls. It had seen numerous floods, and the most recent flood had left everything stored down there wet and molded.

Nevertheless, I didn't care about any of that. Many of my sister's furnishings were stored down there, along with the few items I had brought. You have to picture a storage place, with boxes and items stacked from the floor to the ceiling in some places. Not your usual basement. The first night, I literally slept on boxes. I was mentally and emotionally exhausted.

The next day I got up and started rummaging through the stored belongings to see what I could use. I began to move some things around, and in doing so, I found an old console television that still worked, but I would have to splice into the cable from upstairs, run a new wire down, and hook it up to the television. The belongings included a couple of old recliners, a desk, and several tables I arranged to create a makeshift kitchen area.

After rearranging some things and using what I had to work with, I created a small studio-style apartment amongst the stored items. Not what one would pick when looking for a new place to live, but it brought back some of my childhood memories of the forts that I would build as a kid, which made it just a little bit more comforting.

It allowed me the privacy I needed to maintain just a little of my sanity and independence. My siblings wouldn't allow me to freeload on my parents, though. They insisted that I help out around the house with grocery shopping and help with taking Dad when he needed to go and do inspections. I could do that. It was the least I could do, and it gave me some sort of existence at a time when I was feeling nonexistent.

My computer was the only thing I brought with me, and I set up the old desk that I found and hooked up the computer there by the TV; this is where I spent about eighty-five percent of my time after moving back in. Mom's health had gone downhill after her open-heart surgery, and Dad was still getting around slowly, so my presence helped comfort them. Even if I didn't help, they were comforted knowing I was safe.

I was still going to get Kelli on a pretty regular basis. She liked visiting now that I lived with her Granny and Pop. She was spoiled even more now than ever. She was now old enough to realize that I didn't live in the same place but didn't care where we lived as long as we were able to spend time together. Having her around kept me living a reality. There were so many times that I wanted to check out but couldn't bear the thought of leaving her behind.

My dad was a home inspector at the time after he retired from residential construction, and I was helping drive him around to do his inspections while living there. He would split the fees with me and teach me the ins and outs of the inspection process along the way. This was something that I enjoyed doing, and I had the experience to back me up, so I thought this would be a good direction for me to go.

I used my computer to generate the inspection reports for him and keep track of all the associated invoices. Dad knew nothing about the computer but trusted me to take care of the business end of the inspections and collect the money from the lenders once the loans closed.

I was still indulging in the pain meds, methadone, and whatever else was available, even if all I had was a few extra dollars, and still smoking a little weed when I couldn't find anything else. The pills I could easily do in the privacy of my basement apartment, but I had to sneak out the basement door when I wanted to smoke a little weed. I acted very childish and disrespectful to my parents by taking advantage of their generosity in allowing me to stay with them rent-free.

Still traveling back and forth to Powell County to hang out with the guys up there was becoming a fairly normal routine. Owl was not in very good health, and as far as I knew, he didn't eat very good meals regularly. I would usually go to Powell County after dinner, and if we had any leftovers, Mom would pack them up for me to take to Owl. He was always so grateful for the home-cooked meals. I would hang out with him there at his place and keep him company many times until he fell asleep on the couch, then I would slip out the door and return to Lexington.

This got to be a pretty regular routine for me during the week. Back then, gas was barely a dollar a gallon, so I could put five dollars of gas in the car and make it there and back easily. I would usually bounce between Owl's place and Jackie's, depending on if I needed to get more pills. Jackie had all the good connections and could almost always find something, even if it was just one or two to get me by. He wasn't a dealer by any stretch of the imagination. It's just what friends do for each other in that particular situation.

Meanwhile, back in Lexington, Dad and I was still doing the inspections. The lenders kept us pretty busy, and the checks were still coming in, and as I said before, Dad was splitting those with me to help me get back on my feet, but the checks weren't regular enough to keep up with the daily need for the pain pills and methadone. The methadone helped to ease the sickness when the pain meds weren't available, and more often than not, I would just be satisfied with the methadone because they were much easier to get.

I'm sure that Dad knew of my addiction, maybe he didn't know how deeply involved I was, but he knew. There were some mornings when he would come downstairs and find me slumped over the arm of the desk chair, passed out. I'm sure there were times when he wondered if I was even alive.

Mom, however, refused to admit that her baby was a drug addict. It was her way of dealing with something she didn't believe to be real or totally true. Looking back, she had always been very protective over me; I believe it wasn't just for my protection as much as it was for her being able to cope with it.

It got to the point where I was getting increasingly dependent on pain pills and methadone just to get through the day, and the need for more money was more demanding. I could easily go through a hundred dollars a day, and that was just to keep me motivated enough to get through the day without getting sick. I needed to come up with an alternative income to make up the difference.

At first, I started pawning stuff like the camera we used for the inspections. I would get fifty dollars for the pawn, just enough to get a few dollars of gas to make the trip and enough for a few pills and a pack of smokes. When a check would come in the mail, I would take that and get the camera out of the pawn, then turn right around and do it all again a few days later. This process continued for months, and I even used the same scheme with other items of value, like tools and whatever I could get my hands on. I couldn't allow them to sell the camera, so I was desperate to come up with another plan to get some quick cash. When you're that desperate, your mind can convince you to do things you would normally never even consider doing.

Desperate for new ways to get money, I started watching for the mailman every day in hopes of beating Dad to the mailbox in case there were any checks. If so, I wouldn't always tell him how many checks had come, and sometimes lied if there was only one check and kept it all instead of splitting it with him. There's no way I would have ever done this to my dad if I weren't in a selfish, drug-induced state of mind, but I was just focused on getting a fix.

I hated whom I had become. I wasn't raised to be this way. I was taught to be better than this. Often it seemed as though I was running from myself and whom I had become as much as I was chasing that illusion dream. I was so far removed from reality that I didn't see any way back. I couldn't even imagine what a new start looked like; all I could see was an ending.

It was probably early 2002 by this time, and I was spending more and more time in Powell County. I didn't even want to go back to Lexington and take a chance of missing out on an opportunity to get at least a little something, but I needed money for even the littlest amount of anything, and home was where the best opportunity for money was going to be.

Chapter XVI

The Downfall Begins

When I did go back to Lexington, my nephew Ben would often show up there at the house from time to time. I knew that he usually had some cocaine or at least knew where to get some pretty good stuff. I thought this might be an opportunity to cash in on trading material. I had done plenty of cocaine in the past, and as much as I liked it, I hated it that much more. I couldn't function on that stuff. It was obvious as hell when I was jacked up. My jaws would be like two opposite poles of a magnet avoiding contact with each other, and I never shut up.

I did, however, think I might be able to invest in some really good powder and cut it enough to make a little profit for pills. That, or even trade some of the coke for pills. I didn't really know of any cocaine around Clay City, it was mostly pain pills, and I had never seen so many people on disability in all my life. Eastern Kentucky and Appalachia were known for their pill mills back then. The number of doctors issuing prescriptions for opioids was ridiculous.

I wanted to capitalize on some of those opioids, and cocaine might be the answer. Ben knew the source for the coke, and I had the contacts for sales. After a few trips to Eastern Kentucky, I built a nice little client base, and one day, someone asked me if I knew how to cook it down and make a crack. I had never even heard of such a thing. I had seen people in movies heating it in a spoon for intravenous use, but as for crack, I'd never heard of it.

A crack is a smokable form of cocaine that started becoming popular in the United States around the mid-eighties and ballooned into widespread use in the nineties. That's probably why I hadn't heard much about it. It's a very highly addictive form of cocaine with all of the impurities cooked out of it. The waxy-like substance that remains is what's known as rock cocaine or crack.

I began experimenting with small amounts in a spoon like everyone had explained the process to me; however, that was taking forever to make very much quantity, so I started experimenting with larger quantities and using the microwave. I was blown away by the final results that I got. The spoon method was for tiny amounts, say for intravenous users, but I was more interested in producing the rock form in much bigger quantities.

I needed a quiet place to work on perfecting this process. I wasn't about to do it in my parent's basement, so I talked to a good friend of mine. He agreed to let me use his place because he had all of the appliances, and it was an inconspicuous location that wasn't on the radar of the law, at least not at that particular time. I started with small batches of maybe a gram of powder, then gradually worked my way up to a quarter ounce of powder, then an ounce per batch.

It would easily sell for fifty dollars for a few grams of rock, and I was quadrupling what I paid for the powder in hours. This stuff was blowing up this small Eastern Kentucky town. All they had known to this point was pills and weed, and the pills were getting hard to come by, so people were at the house around the clock every time I would cook up a batch. It was so crazy at times that we had to lock the doors and close all the curtains to get a break.

I was going through a couple of ounces of powder every couple of days, and resupplying meant I had to make another trip back to Lexington to see my guy. Running on literally zero sleep for days at a time and driving back and forth to Lexington every few days was taxing on my body and taking a very big gamble on getting caught in

53

the process. Yeah, I thought about the police, but the drive to keep going was more overpowering than the fear of getting caught.

There were a couple of really close calls on the trips back and forth to Lexington to re-up. Once, I was entering the parkway and must have dozed off and run off the shoulder of the road and over-corrected and spun the truck thrice in the middle of the road. How I kept from rolling it was beyond me, and thank God there wasn't any traffic, or it could have ended so much worse than it did.

Another time, I was traveling back to Lexington on very little sleep, dozed off again in a construction area, and wiped out about five of those big orange barrels on the edge of the road. One was lodged under the front of the truck, and I dragged it along. Looking back on some of those situations, it is obvious that God was watching out for me, or it could have been much worse.

Somehow, I didn't feel threatened while I was at the house. I mean, let's keep it real. They could have busted through the doors any time and caught me with enough product and cash to put me away without a trial. Maybe it was because of the location and the homeowner's connection with law enforcement that kept them at bay. I don't know with any certainty why they never came in on me, but it somehow gave me a sense of power and arrogance.

I know that they had to know something was going on because of the traffic in and out of there every day. People began showing up mostly under cover of darkness, but eventually, they couldn't stay away, not even in broad daylight. I don't mean to sound like I'm bragging about all that I did, but if you continue on this journey with me, you have to realize exactly where I was mentally and emotionally every step of the way.

I also realize that if you are reading this and have gone through something similar, or currently are, some of this context may wake up too many memories for you. If so, it is not my intention at all to cause you discomfort in our journey together, and I pray that you can find some comfort and peace from being on this journey with me.

With that being said, by this time, I was getting some strange people showing up at the house. Before this, a rotating group of people usually gathered around the kitchen table with a pile of rocks in the center. If they didn't bring their own pipe, I had extra. For me, it was a social time. Once I sold enough to recover my cost and enough to resupply, it was party time. I'd throw a bag on the table, and everyone would participate.

I started noticing people constantly peeping out the blinds all the time. They were freaking me out. It was like the stuff increased their ability to hear even the smallest sounds blocks away. And then they would whisper to everyone at the table. I was like, what the hell is going on with you people? Why are you acting like that?

And then there was the crawling around on the floor looking for tiny pieces that they thought they had dropped under the table. 'Stop doing that,' I said. 'We have a table full of the product here, and you're down on the floor crawling around looking for hope. I'd never seen anything like it before, and it was very annoying. I didn't understand what made them act like this. It was very creepy. I had smoked a lot of rock and never acted like that. It just didn't make any sense to me, at least not at the time.

It was about the same time that I met Teresa. She lived just up the street from where I was staying and was a regular client for a while. She was married but separated and a big flirt. She played me like a Tennessee fiddle. For an old guy like me, this was very flattering to have a much younger female coming on to me, and I fell for it hook, line and sinker. She started hanging around the house more and more and working her way into the inner circle where I hadn't let anyone near me for the most part.

I was pretty protective of my feelings, but I let my guard down with her for whatever reason. She was very good at manipulating the truth to make it work in her favor and using what she had to get what she wanted. I hadn't given any thought to relationships in a long time. After the last divorce, I didn't think I would ever put myself in that position again. I still hadn't really dealt with the pain; I only pushed it down below the surface with all the other stuff and just kept going.

Things were starting to become different around the house, and I was growing increasingly uncomfortable with the situation that I had once been at ease with. Tensions were higher than ever before, and I believe it had much to do with my relationship with Teresa. The people I once trusted warned me to be careful, but I didn't want to hear it, and I began to push my friends away.

One night, after a really long day of partying, one of my good friends hanging around all day was starting to geek out. I had already put away what little stash I had left to sell and was really needing to lay down for a while. He was begging me to front him another bag, but I told him that he had had enough and it was time for him to go to the house and crash for a while. He eventually left, but just a few minutes later, he returned to the door and said he just wanted to apologize for his actions.

We walked into the kitchen, and when he started to talk, I could see the rage building in his eyes, and in the blink of an eye, out of nowhere, he swung his elbow and caught me on the side of my face and knocked me to the ground. I freaked out as he lunged for me, and I dove under the kitchen table to get away from him. It was the only way out of the kitchen, and I ran to the recliner where I knew there was a pistol, grabbed it, and ran out the front door to gather my wits and figure out what had just happened.

I was trying to figure out what the hell was wrong with this guy. I'd known him for a while and never had seen anything like this before. He had lost his freaking mind. I was prepared to shoot him if he came out of the house at me again. It was then that I realized that everything I had was still in the house, and so was he. I had to get in there and get him away from it to retrieve my bag with my stuff. I got a friend on the phone and got him to come over and calm him down and get him out of the house.

I just knew that when I was able to get back in the house, my stuff would be gone, but little to my surprise, it was all still there. I seriously don't think he came back to rob me; he just wanted to kick my butt for disrespecting him and telling him to go home and chill. I was across the street at another friend's house while they got him calmed down and out of the house. The next morning, he returned to the house again to apologize. I talked to him through the door (with the pistol nearby in my waistband), and I believe his apology was sincere, and just like that, we were back to our usual selves.

After that little incident, Owl became uncomfortable with the situation and asked me to look for a different place to conduct business. He wasn't mad at me, but this was his home, and he wasn't even staying there anymore because of all the drama and late-night traffic. He was a sick man recovering from cancer, and I had come into his home, turned it into a madhouse, and run him out. He didn't see it that way, though. He would have given me the shirt off of his back, that's just how he was, but I knew it was time for me to go, and I started looking for other options.

Chapter XVII

Tensions Are Building

By this time, I had stopped returning to my parents' house. I stayed in eastern Kentucky every day and only traveled back to Lexington when I needed to resupply. I felt safe there and wouldn't even leave unless I had to make another supply run. I would give people money to go and grab us some food and bring it to the house. The paranoia was taking a toll on me emotionally and physically. I was starting to understand why everyone would peek out the windows whenever they heard a noise.

Dad would call me to see if I could come in and help with inspections, which were falling off and not as plentiful as they had been in the few years before this, but I would make up excuses why I couldn't get back in. The sad part is that I was driving his vehicle that we had been using for inspections, so either one of my siblings or I would have to take him. Neither of my parents was driving anymore by then, so they relied a hundred percent on one of us kids to help get them where they needed to go, but I was continuously letting them down.

I was so caught up in the chaos of keeping it all going that the guilt wouldn't allow me to go back and face my family. I missed Christmas with the family that year and even my uncle's funeral. By this time, my family knew something was seriously wrong, but the more they tried to communicate with me, the more I turned away and avoided them. They didn't understand what I was going through. None of them had ever been in serious trouble with the law, let alone experimented with drugs, so empathizing with me was impossible.

Kelli and her mom were living in Stanton, the next town over from where I had been staying, so I could see her off and on. I didn't want her to be around the activity that I was involved in, so I would usually take some time away from it and spend some time with her. Jamie was now twenty and doing his own thing. I hadn't been back to Versailles since I left after being evicted from my house, so I didn't see him much anymore. We talked on the phone occasionally, but that was about it.

I remember times when people asked me to meet them on some country road to make a drop. At the time, it seemed like just another routine deal, out away from the watchful eye of the law, but looking back on it now, I can easily see where it could have been meant as a setup. There were places in those mountains where a man could easily end up missing and never be found. I was very trusting of the people I dealt with regularly, probably more so than I should have been because someone so desperate for a fix might do just about anything when given the right opportunity.

Desperate for a place to stay with ease of access for my clients and somewhere with a little protection, I got a room at a small motel there just outside of town near the interstate. I could easily hop on the interstate to make a Lexington run. It was a nice little place, so it drew no unwanted attention. I knew the owner, and he kept to himself and didn't ask many questions, so it made for a quiet little place to set up a temporary shop. I'm unsure if he didn't know what was happening or didn't want to know. Either way, I think as long as he got his rent for the room, he minded his own business.

One day, right in broad daylight, I heard a banging on the door. At least, I thought it was my door, but it turned out it was actually the door next to mine. When I peeked out of the curtains, I saw multiple law enforcement lined up along the unit wall; guns were drawn, calling for the occupant next door to come out. It turned out they were serving a warrant for the guy next door. You talk about soiling yourself. There I sat with a table full of the product I was packaging, paraphernalia and stacks of cash, and by now, drawers full of crap.

I was so freaked out that I didn't even try to flush anything or get rid of any evidence. For all that I knew, they were coming after me next. They had been cracking down a lot lately on small-time dealers, and they had to know I was there because everyone knows everything in a small town. My truck wasn't there; I kept it at another location and had different people drop me off there so I wouldn't draw attention. People knew my blazer; if it were there, they would beat down the doors all day and night.

I knew it was just a matter of time before the law caught up to me, but that didn't matter much. In a way, I would push my luck until it ran out. By this time, I was barely selling enough to re-up and partying on the rest. When you have so much at your disposal, keeping up with what you've done and what you have to sell is hard. I was becoming short on money more often and running out of excuses for not having it all when I went to re-up. I had to set up a few smaller distributors around the area to help get rid of enough to cover costs, or it would disappear, and I'd be left with nothing.

Eager to keep the business between us going, my supplier let me slide more than he really should have. He didn't know I was cooking the powder or smoking most of it myself. He warned me initially not to get involved in that because he knew how dangerously addictive it was, so I was very careful not to let him know anything about my dealings. The business had begun to slow down a little because I had shown so many people how to cook that they were doing it themselves, or at least trying, but they were failing miserably.

Eventually, we had to leave the motel and find another place. By this time, it was Teresa and me, and she said her dad's house was available. Her brother and his girlfriend stayed there, but there was room enough for us to crash there too. Her dad was living with his girlfriend, so we decided to hang out there for a while and lay low. I was also running low on powder and out of money, so re-supplying wasn't an option. I had called my guy and told him that I had been in jail in another county for unrelated charges, which wasn't the truth at all, just a smokescreen to buy some time because I still owed him some money.

Chapter XVIII

The Raid

This was probably late December 2002, and the walls were closing in on me fast. I was finding myself in a place I had never been before emotionally. On the one hand, I had a nice place to stay at my parent's house if I wanted, but the desire to be near any possible opportunity for a fix was all I wanted. With nothing left to pawn, I turned to my last resort, which was burnt-up chores. The chore was a specific type of Brillo pad used to put in the stem (pipe) to catch the liquid when the rock melted; when it heated up, it would procure the smoke. There's nothing more exhilarating than the sound of the rock melting and the rush of smoke filling your lungs. It's a feeling you chase every time you hit the stem, and it's never quite the same as that first time, but your mind convinces you to keep trying.

Over time, I just collected all the burnt chores and saved them in a jar because I knew you could extract the oils from them. I had even saved the leftover water from when I did a run because I knew that it contained small amounts of cooled oils. I never really had to resort to going back to these resources, but desperate times call for desperate measures. These resources lasted a little while but eventually ran dry too. We got our hands on a small amount of low-grade product there locally, but the quality wasn't good enough to cook up.

Teresa's dad was always stopping by the house intoxicated and looking for a little bit of rock, and we kept telling him that we didn't have anything, but he wasn't falling for that. He thought he knew better, especially when he was drinking; he wouldn't take no for an answer. He would show up all hours of the day and night, banging on the door. We changed the locks to keep him from just walking in on us, but all that did was piss him off, and one night in early January 2003, he was pretty persistent in trying to get in that he threatened to get the state police and come back. We just blew him off as we had with his threats many times before.

I was awakened very early the next morning by yelling and banging on the door. I assumed it was her dad still pissed off and again wanting in. The next thing I knew, the door flew open, and cops came flooding in, yelling, "Search warrant!" Barely awake, I hadn't even had time to wrap my head around what was going on when they were in our room and had us pinned to the bed, slapping the handcuffs on everyone. Knowing we didn't have any product, I wasn't all that worried. Basically, all they had on us was possession of paraphernalia and maybe some residue from some stems and a few stray pills.

There were city police officers, state police and DEA digging through everything, looking for what they thought we had. Most likely, acting on a tip from her dad, they thought that I had the mother's lode and were determined to find it. I wasn't all that worried because I knew I didn't have anything. Luckily, everything I did had been distributed to my people, but they were determined. They kept putting pressure on us to tell them where it was, and they weren't taking no for an answer.

They eventually separated us and took me outside on the front porch and took turns trying to pressure me into talking. I kept trying to assure them that there wasn't anything in the house or my truck sitting in the driveway. I told them that if anyone should be held responsible, it should be me. I didn't want Teresa, her brother and his girlfriend to go to jail. I told them I would take full responsibility for whatever they found if they let everyone else go.

After about an hour of searching through the house, they eventually wrapped it up, took me downtown to the station for more questioning, and booked me into the jail. Somehow, I knew this day would eventually come, but you're never prepared for that kind of invasion that early in the morning. Based on the amount of physical evidence they found, like my accounts book, they charged me with trafficking in a controlled substance, possession of drug paraphernalia and a controlled substance in an improper container (Methadone and Xanax).

The book I kept with me at all times had my client's initials, and beside them, it had what they owed me, what they had paid, and the date they paid me. Plenty of people's names from the community were listed in that book—names that would have raised some eyebrows if the list had been made public. That was my biggest downfall and the most incriminating evidence they had on me. I didn't think that was very incriminating, though. It could have meant anything, but they weren't stupid. I knew they had been watching me for a while, just waiting for the right time to pounce on me.

Once I was booked into the little county jail, they put me in a cell with many familiar faces. Most of the guys there had been a client of mine at one point or another. Their initials were probably listed in that book. It was a little bit of a relief because I wasn't really sure what to expect from a small-town jail, but the guys briefed me on the protocol and hooked me up with the essentials because the guard hadn't given me anything when they booked me in. It had been a very long day, and I was still sick from all that had transpired since that morning. So, all I wanted to do was just sleep.

I didn't want to tell my family about my arrest, but I also didn't want to sit there in that jail. It stunk and was nasty. There weren't any bunks available, so naturally, the new guy had to make a bedroll on the floor, and for an old guy with back problems, that wasn't very comfortable. I eventually got up the nerve to call my sister, told her about the arrest, and asked her to get the money together to bond me

64

out. Much to my dismay, but not surprised, she told me that she thought I needed to take this time to think about why I was there.

Teresa and her brother weren't arrested, and she told me that she would try and get some money together to bond me out since I had taken all of the charges and asked them not to charge them with anything. In a small town like that, the district court was only held once a week and the circuit court once a month, so the process there would drag on forever. I remember my first court appearance when I was arraigned. I walked into the courtroom and looked around, hoping to see a familiar face, but to my disappointment, nobody was there.

Just a few short months before that, I was the most popular guy in the county, and now I stood there alone to face the judge as he read me my charges. Humiliated wasn't the word to describe how I felt then. I didn't expect any of my family to be there for the arraignment, but there's always that small piece of you that holds out hope that someone would show up without moral support. If not my family, at least Teresa, but she didn't even show up either. It didn't take long for me to realize this would be a long, dark and lonely journey. I wasn't in any mental state of mind to deal with this, but I knew I wasn't going anywhere any time soon.

One night during my stay there, two guys overpowered one of the guards and busted out of jail. Apparently, they had been planning this for some time, and when the time was right, they knocked on the cell door and asked for some clean towels. When the guard opened the door to hand them the towels, they grabbed his arm, slung him into the cell, ran out, slammed the door, and locked him in it. They knew that when the guard opened the door, he would leave the keys in it, so it was just a matter of catching him off guard and making their move.

Remember that this is a very small County jail, and I believe he was the only guard on duty at the time and one other female deputy that worked in the intake area. They managed to take her by surprise, opened another cell to let another friend out, grabbed the keys to a vehicle and escaped right out the front door.

Meanwhile, the guard was still in the cell with the rest of us. He was banging on the cell door for someone to let him out. By that time, the entire jail had erupted in yelling and banging. Everyone was hoping they would let them out as well, and if they were smart, they would have, then the authorities would be looking for thirty people instead of three.

They were all caught within just a few days and returned to jail, but they were all separated this time. I don't think they had any plan for when they made it out. Perhaps they never expected to get that far and hadn't planned what to do if the plan worked. That was the craziest thing I had ever witnessed—just another day in Powell County paradise.

Chapter XIX

Bonded Out

It was a long thirty days in that hell hole of jail before I made bond and got out. Teresa and my sister went in together to come up with enough to make the bond, and you would have thought that I would have high-tailed it out of that crazy place and headed for the safety of my parent's house, but no, I headed straight to Teresa's house. While I was in jail, she had managed to rent a duplex, and I never gave it a second thought as to how she managed to get a place. I was just glad to be out, and the first thing that I asked was if she knew where we could get anything.

I tried to contact some of my connections in the area, but nobody wanted to talk to me. Word on the street was that I had turned state evidence on everyone in that little book, and nobody would even give me the time of day. Of course, that wasn't the case; they were all just paranoid and couldn't figure out how I got out so quickly. The streets can turn on you quickly when you are in a bad situation.

Besides my brother-in-law Jackie, only one guy who had been my right-hand man and biggest distributor would have anything to do with me after my release or even be seen talking to me. At one point, I was the man to know in that small town, and now I couldn't find a friend. Even Teresa had become questionable, and I had a gut feeling that it didn't sit well with me. I suspected she was seeing someone else, but she kept me close enough to keep me on her good side because I took the charges and kept her out of jail.

I eventually went to stay with my friend Chad and his family because he was a good source to score just enough to keep me from getting sick. He still owed me a little bit of money from before I was arrested, so I crashed on his living room floor for a few days while I tried to figure out my next move. One night, while staying with Chad, I woke up in excruciating pain in my chest. I was positive that I had a heart attack. Teresa was the only person I could reach at that time of the night, so she came and picked me up and drove me to Winchester to the emergency room.

I remember walking into the emergency room and collapsing in the middle of the floor. I didn't remember anything else until I woke up in a hospital room the next morning. My sister was there and told me what had happened. I was diagnosed with an infected gallbladder and multiple gallstones. I remember having a similar episode while in the Powell County jail, but nothing as serious as this one. They treated me for acid reflux, which was its end. I hadn't had any more complications since then, but apparently, it was much worse than the acid reflux they first thought.

Without medical insurance, they wouldn't perform any surgery unless I could pay out of pocket, and that wouldn't happen. I tried searching for assistance from a program that the hospital recommended, but with credit as bad as mine, well, that wasn't even an option, so I carried on the best I could and just tried to keep from doing anything that would aggravate it and hope for the best. After I was released from the hospital, I thought it best to go back to my parents' house, recuperate the best I could, and try to find some assistance with the surgery.

Meanwhile, I still have to travel back to Powell County for court once a month. Just protocol for the most part while getting through the district court phase of the process. With my trafficking charges, I was facing a class C felony charge and would have to go through the process of the district court and then see if the grand jury thought that they had enough evidence to indict me and then start the process all over again in circuit court. The court was only held once a month, so the process dragged on for what seemed like an eternity, but at least I was out on bond while awaiting the outcome.

The grand jury indicted me on the charges, and the process started again in circuit court. One day, I showed up for court, called my attorney to check in before court, and he told me that I wasn't on the docket that day. I knew that I was scheduled, but after he did some checking, he came back and told me that I was, in fact, not on the docket and to keep my mouth shut and not to say anything to anyone else about it. I went into court and sat through the whole day to make sure, but I was never called up. By this time, I am dumbfounded by what has just transpired.

On the one hand, I didn't want to get myself into any more trouble than I already was, but on the other hand, I wasn't about to do their job for them. My attorney told me after court that day that my paperwork was missing and to go home and wait to hear from him. He told me that if I didn't hear from him not to show up for court. That was it. No other explanation. What the hell just happened? Are you kidding me? My paperwork goes missing, and nobody knows anything about my case. However weird that may sound, it was real, and I got in the truck and got the hell out of town as fast as I could.

My suspicions about Teresa seeing someone else proved to be true, and I didn't have much contact with her after that. By that time, I was trying to get through each day. I remember stopping by Chad's house one day looking for anything to get by on because I was just so sick. I was at the lowest point I had ever been by this time. Daytime wasn't so bad, but the nights were dark and lonely. I remember telling Chad that I had someone that wanted a few grams, and he let me have what he had left to go and make the sale.

That was as far from the truth as one could be. I didn't have anyone wanting to make a purchase; I just wanted to get one more fix at whatever the cost. I remember driving just outside of town, turning down a gravel road, and driving to the end. I parked the truck, reclined the seat back, and dropped rock after rock into the stem, trying my best to overdose. I was done with living. I didn't own a gun or would have used it that day to end my life. The more I tried to overdose, the more I realized it wouldn't happen, and I would have to answer Chad for what I had done.

I stayed back there for what seemed like hours. It was nearly dark by the time I left, dreading facing reality, and even worse, I would have to face another long night alone. I didn't know how much more of this I could take. You don't see a way out when you are in a place like that. Starting over isn't an option. You expect an end, and you know it's eventually coming, but you don't know when.

Everyone who loves you begs you to stop the destructive lifestyle, but how do you walk away? It's not a matter of quitting because half of the battle you fight is in your head, and as unfortunate as it is, you don't just walk away from that. I hoped to get court-appointed drug treatment from my case, but even that fell through, so now I don't know where to turn. I couldn't ask anyone for help because I didn't think they knew what to do to help me. I didn't even know what would work. All I knew was that I was tired and wanted it to end.

Chapter XX

Lexington Arrest

By the summer of 2003, I was spending more time at my parents' house again while trying to figure out how to get some assistance with the gallbladder surgery. Pain pills and methadone were so hard to find, and that just heightened the pressure to come up with different ways to get my hands on some cash. It was becoming more obvious that I wasn't going to be able to get the surgery, so I continued to self-medicate and tried to avoid spicy foods.

That basement was my refuge. I hardly ever came out of it when I was there, only to go upstairs to grab something to eat, and even then, I would take it back down there to eat. It was my safe place. It wasn't the greatest accommodation, but it was where I felt most comfortable, and that was huge for me at that time. I needed that place of comfort. I had found a new connection closer to home, so anytime I could get a little cash, I'd give him a call.

By this time, there was just enough money coming in to score a twenty-dollar rock occasionally or a few pills when they were available. I couldn't live like this anymore. The obsession with needing something to get me through the day was heavy on me emotionally, and I was so tired of trying to survive.

Mom was dealing with congestive heart failure issues after her open-heart surgery, and Dad's health wasn't all that great at the time, either. Instead of spending quality time with them in their later years,

I chose to withdraw to my refuge, where I could be alone. Alone was where I felt most comfortable. I couldn't deal with the pressure to perform normal daily activities like helping care for my elderly parents, who lived right there in the same house.

If you've ever dealt with addiction or loved someone who was or currently is, you know it does not come and go. It is daily. Your mind never rests. The psychological side of addiction is very dangerous to the addict and those around you. I guess you could say I was fortunate in some ways because my addiction wasn't hard-core intravenous heroin or meth use. I was fine with crushing up some pills to snort or smoking a little weed. Alcohol wasn't even a factor at this point in my journey because I could function on the pills, but alcohol prevented me from functioning and getting around when I needed to.

I can't help but think back now and be thankful that we didn't have the drugs available to us then that is widespread on the streets today. The fentanyl would have killed me because I never checked the validity of a pill back then, they weren't laced with fentanyl, and when pills were available, they were legit. They weren't manufactured in someone's garage or makeshift laboratory in a warehouse somewhere. My heart aches for anyone struggling with addiction in this day and time. I know their struggle is much more than anything I experienced throughout my journey.

Among all the stored items in the basement were a lot of Dad's business items from the office he closed when he retired. I came across an old checkbook from Dad's business, and as far as I knew, the bank had changed hands or was no longer even a legit bank anymore. Nevertheless, the ideas started rolling in my head.

I considered whether or not I could pull off cashing one to get some quick cash, but my nerves hadn't caught up with my desperation at that point. So, all I did was toss around ideas on how to pull something like that off. The checkbook was a business checkbook, so I thought I could use Dad's typewriter to type out one of the checks, forge Dad's signature, and take it to the bank where Mom and Dad had an account to see if they would cash it for me.

The bank was used to seeing me, and Dad both come in regularly to cash inspection checks, so they knew me by name and for all they knew, I was to be trusted like any other customer with an account. I got up the nerve to try it one day. I planned to play stupid if they asked any questions about the check; worst case, I could tell them I would take the check back and have them write me another check from a different account. To my complete surprise, the teller went through the normal routine and cashed the check for two hundred fifty dollars without question. I couldn't believe it.

I was so surprised that paranoia soon took over, and I was convinced that the bank would call Dad to inquire about the check that was cashed against his account. For the moment, though, I had the cash in my hand and quickly made the trip east to my trusted source for a few pills and a little partying for the weekend. It's amazing how much difference a little money can make you feel mentally, even after feeling like the whole world was crashing in on me just a few hours before. Just the thought of having the money and being on my way to getting some relief already made me feel better.

For the next several days, I listened in on any incoming phone calls to make sure it wasn't the bank calling, and I even made a point to get to the mailbox before Dad did so I could catch any notices from the bank about the check I had cashed. To my surprise, the phone call or notices never came. Was I that lucky, or had the bank just not caught on to me yet? Either way, I figured since I got away with it once, surely, I could do it again, so I did, and it worked again.

The checkbook didn't have many checks in it, maybe a dozen, so I knew that this asset wouldn't last much longer, but I had decided to keep pushing my luck until it or the checks ran out. I managed to go through the remaining checks over the next several weeks, except for one. For whatever reason, I left that last check in the book. Maybe it was paranoia setting in, or maybe fate had a different plan in mind.

Church wasn't even on my radar anymore. I couldn't even remember the last time I had been to church at that point. I didn't feel worthy of God and had long since thought He had turned His back on me. You tell yourself that you need to get it together before you can think about going to church. And besides, they would probably pick up on you immediately if you walked into a church in that condition and asked you to leave. These are the things your mind convinces you of, but the devil is a liar! The enemy comes to kill, steal and destroy, and he had done a pretty good job with all of the above on me.

That summer, an elderly lady contacted Dad about installing a new roof on the house he had built for her and her husband twenty years ago. I had done a lot of these jobs for him that people had called about through the years as side jobs, so I was familiar with the process, and it was usually a quick dollar, so I told Dad that I would take on the job and talk to her and give her a price for the work.

I contacted her and met with her to look at the job. It was a straightforward re-roof; I subcontracted the job to a roofer and added a little on the back end for my services. I gave her the price and asked for half the money upfront to deliver the materials. That was my procedure every time I contracted a job like this, and she trusted my dad, so she was okay with writing the check.

I had every intention of ordering the materials for the job, but when I took the check to the bank and cashed it, something inside me clicked, and I immediately got on the phone and started making calls looking for anything I could find. Needless to say, little by little, I went through the money pretty fast. Always telling myself, just one more time and then I will take the rest and get the materials for the job. I didn't go into this looking to take advantage of this little old lady, and I kept telling myself that I would get it done for her; I just never did.

She began calling Dad, asking when we were coming to work on the house, and I kept using the excuse that the roofer was backed up and as soon as he got caught up, we would get right on her job. That never happened. In fact, I had never even contacted a roofer yet. Her daughter started calling, asking about it after a while. Still, I just kept avoiding her and putting off the inevitable until she left a message saying she was contacting a lawyer. She did that, and I was subpoenaed to court for a civil lawsuit. I showed up for the first court date and was ordered by the court to pay the full amount back, plus court costs.

Immediately upon hearing what the judge had to say, when I turned to walk back to my seat, two sheriff deputies approached me and told me that I was being detained for a failure to appear to warrant out of Powell County. I was floored! I didn't have any court dates that I knew of because I never did hear back from my attorney there. I was placed in a holding cell and later transported back to Powell County. I was afraid that this would cause the judge in that case to revoke my bond, and I would be held until trial.

The next morning, a Powell County deputy came to Lexington and got me and took me back to Powell County to await my court appearance on the failure to appear warrant. After I got back to the Powell County jail, I immediately started trying to contact my attorney to tell him what had happened and find out why I was suddenly back in court, given the fact that a few months earlier, they had supposedly lost all of my paperwork. My attorney was just as surprised as I was to hear about the new court date and was able to get me released back out on my original bond until the next scheduled court date.

It turned out that the grand jury that had indicted me on my charges had met again, and originally, they didn't charge Teresa with anything when I was arrested. Still, they decided there was enough evidence to indict her as well, and when she found out that she was being charged, my paperwork mysteriously showed back up. It makes one wonder who was behind the disappearance from the beginning. I think maybe she was caught up in some other activity, and the grand jury was already looking at her in another case and decided that they had enough to indict her on that previous incident as well.

By this time, the summer of 2003 was winding down. My case in Powell County was still dragging along, but I didn't care because that meant that any jail or prison time, if any, would be further away. I didn't think I would do any serious time for those charges. I seriously thought I could get the charges reduced in a last-minute plea agreement with the prosecution to maybe possession of paraphernalia and maybe some court-appointed drug rehab or something. I didn't take it very seriously at all.

My resources were quickly running out, and still desperate enough to get a little more cash, I had to devise another plan. Remember that one last check I mentioned that was left in the checkbook? Well, for whatever reason, nothing had yet come of all those other checks that I had written, and then I remembered that there was still one more check left. Enough time had elapsed that I was sure that the bank was onto me by now, so I had to think of an alternative place that was a good source to cash third-party checks.

Ben had stopped by the house one morning, and I had already typed out and signed the check, so when I told him that I had a check to get cashed, he assumed it was just another inspection check and asked if he could ride along.

I told Ben there wasn't enough in my parent's account to cover this check, so we would have to find a liquor store to cash it for me. There were plenty of liquor stores nearby, so I just picked one at random and gave it a shot. The first stop didn't work out. The guy working the counter didn't know me, so he said he couldn't cash it, so he went on to the next stop.

The second liquor store we stopped at seemed a little more promising because the guy at the counter said he'd have to get the money from the back room. While I waited, I made small talk with another patron in the store. The guy returned and said he just needed me to sign the back of the check, so I took care of that for him, and he returned to the back room again. Still hopeful that he was returning with the cash, he seemed to be taking a very long time.

By now, I was starting to get nervous and even considered walking out, when just about that time, the front door opened and in walked a uniformed officer. He immediately walked up to me, and I noticed the guy was now back behind the counter. The officer pointed at me and looked at the guy behind the counter, and he shook his head yes as if he were confirming that I was the one. The officer asked me a couple of questions about the check and where I got it. I tried to lie my way out of it, but it was obvious that I wasn't getting out of it.

Well, as my luck would have it, the owner of this liquor store was a former detective and had seen a lot of bad checks and knew his stuff when it came to deadbeats like me trying to cash a check for a rather large sum of money. When he walked me out of the store, I realized that another officer had taken Ben out of the car and was also questioning him. He was clueless about the check, but when the officer frisked him, he found his stem in his pocket.

Reality had started setting in very fast on the ride to the jail. Ben and I were in the same car, but neither of us said anything the whole trip. I wanted to apologize for him being part of it, especially since he had done nothing wrong other than possessing a stem, but with his history, it wouldn't be easy for him to get out of. He had his share of run-ins with the law, but he always managed to get a break and never really had to serve any hard time. I still felt bad for him for being caught up in my mess.

Chapter XXI

Lexington Jail

When we arrived at the Fayette County Detention Center, it was overwhelming for me, to say the least. The last time I did jail time in Lexington was at the old downtown jail. It was an extremely overcrowded old, seven-story building right in the heart of downtown Lexington. As you drove up to the entrance, the new facility located out Old Frankfort Pike in Lexington looked more like a barn. The actual jail was underground. Everything above ground was offices and administration, but the jail was below ground, and it was huge.

I was booked in and charged with possessing a forged instrument (check) and drug paraphernalia. Not serious charges by themselves, but when you factor in that I was currently out on bond in another county, the reality was, I wasn't getting out anytime soon. I wasn't sure if they were keeping me there or if Powell County would get me and take me back there. I did get to make a phone call to my sister. Not to ask her to try and get me out because I knew that wasn't an option, but to let her know where I was so, they wouldn't worry.

Intake seemed to take forever before they got me dressed and sent me to a cell. There was a specific part of the jail where they held incoming inmates waiting for their arraignment hearing. A single cell was good because I was sick when I got there. All I wanted to do was sleep, but I couldn't even manage to do that. I tried to cry, but nothing worked. It's like my emotions were locked up or nonexistent anymore.

I had suppressed my emotions for so long that there was nothing when I needed to let them out.

I knew this day would eventually come; it was only a matter of time at the rate I was going. I would have given anything to be anywhere other than where I was. I knew this was my new reality, but I couldn't see myself ever getting used to this. I was already experiencing withdrawal sickness before the arrest, and knowing no possible relief was coming hit me hard.

I was housed on the second floor of the pod, and when they opened the cell door to let me out to go down and get chow, I seriously considered the possibility of jumping off the second floor's balcony. I figured that would only end up hurting me even more than I already was. I was just desperate to put an end to this as quickly as possible. My mind wasn't capable of dealing with everything that was happening. This was all new to me, and I didn't have any idea from day to day what was coming next. That was hard because I had gotten so used to the everyday lifestyle that I had been living, and now my life and mind were upside down.

I've read that half of the addiction battle is in your mind. Once you get past the physical sickness of withdrawals and get your system cleaned of the toxins, the next battle is physiological, convincing your mind that you don't need the stimulants to feel normal. I couldn't even remember how long it had been since I hadn't relied on some mind-altering stimulant just to make me feel alive. Twenty-five years, that's how long it had been. I had just turned forty-five years old the month before, and I was about twenty years old when I first started experimenting with various drugs.

I think I spent several days in that cell before my video arraignment when I went before the judge to hear my charges and get the process officially underway. Later that day, they moved me to my new home for the next several months. I didn't see Ben again after our arrest. I had no idea whether or not they even kept him or if they allowed him to bond out. We were arrested on separate charges, so I assumed he could bond out.

The pod I was assigned held about a dozen beds, and I was only one of three white guys in there. The rest were Mexican, and none were fluent in English, so the communication barrier would prove interesting at best.

Don't get me wrong, I have nothing against the Hispanic community, but that music they played on the TV all day long was taxing on my sanity, to say the least. They ruled the TV because they held the majority in the pod, so if it was on, it was tuned to the Telemundo (Hispanic) channel. All those songs seemed happy and upbeat, and I just wasn't in the right frame of mind for all of that.

I stayed to myself at first while I learned the system's routine, and the guys in the pod were really helpful in trying to communicate with me, even with the language barrier. They seemed to all know each other, like a big family. I didn't know if it was because they had been locked up together long enough to make friends or if they knew each other outside. This was my first interaction with Hispanics this personal, so I didn't have any idea. One of the younger guys liked the bald spot on top of my head, so he nicknamed me "sunroof." Say that while rolling the letter "r," and you have it.

I didn't have any money on my account for commissary, so most of the guys in the pod were nice enough to take me in and care for some basic needs until I could get up the nerve to ask my family for a little financial help. Yes, the jail provided everyone with the basics like a tiny bar of soap, a toothbrush and one roll of toilet paper each week, but I soon learned the importance of a roll of toilet paper in jail. It was used for virtually everything. To wipe with, tissue for blowing your nose and napkins at chow, not to mention lining the toilet seat when you had to sit. You got a washcloth, a towel, a bedroll and a box that slid under your bunk to keep your personal items in if you were fortunate to have any.

A far cry from the lifestyle I had grown up with, but this was my new reality. It wasn't the best of accommodations, but you must mentally force your mind to accept it because your opinion doesn't mean anything to anyone in jail. Our pod was one of a dozen others in that particular unit, and they all had solid windows that faced the common area in the center, so any time anything went on in the unit, you could pretty much see, and I saw plenty. Disagreements over a card game or a game of dominos were the cause of most of the fights in the unit.

Shakedowns were demeaning to the spirit. The guards trashed through everything important to you, and anything they considered contraband was tossed out and hauled out with the trash. Shakedowns often included demoralizing strip searches. Not a pat down like you would get upon being arrested; this was just what the term 'strip down' suggested. Stripped down naked one by one in the toilet area of the pod and were told to squat and cough. This is done to see if you have anything hidden in your cavity. It would prove to be very common during my stay, but you never really get comfortable with it.

Detoxing from opioids isn't a pleasant experience, especially when locked up and forced to be without. As I mentioned earlier, I was very fortunate not to have experienced heroin or some of the synthetic forms of opiates that are available today, like fentanyl, or I surely wouldn't have made it out alive. Coming off of them is taxing on your body, especially for a guy like me in his mid-forties.

I'd been a smoker for all of my adult life, and the opioids, smoking, and smoking the rock had taken its toll on my lungs over the long haul. I wouldn't find out the seriousness of that until several years down the road, but I could tell my body wasn't what it used to be and recovering from anything wasn't a pleasant experience.

All of the snorting of cocaine and pills over the years had taken its toll on my sinuses, and most of my teeth were beginning to rot from the inside out. All the years of grinding my jaw teeth had caused some of them to break off, and the pain from the exposed nerves was often unbearable. I saw the jailhouse dentist on occasion and had the worst ones pulled. It was free, so I took advantage of the opportunity; plus, it got me out of my cell for a brief time occasionally.

A couple of months had passed since my arrest, and I was still unable to sleep through the night (or day, for that matter, because all you did in jail was sleep your time away). As long as I was awake, the war in my mind continued every single day. The other symptoms of withdrawal include diarrhea and vomiting. I couldn't keep anything in for any length of time.

The food was terrible, even on a good day. Everything was either boiled or baked, and nothing was sweetened or spiced much at all. I guess it was nutritionally good, but for someone that hadn't practiced nutritious meal planning in a very long time, topped off with the withdrawal from the opioids, it wasn't a good mix. My body was struggling with managing the new diet, to say the least.

I had to retrain my mind to think differently. I had to take notice of triggers that caused my thoughts to react negatively and try to overcome the desire to act out against whatever triggered it. This wasn't that easy to do when you're locked up with a unit full of guys who liked to stay up all night playing cards and then wanted to sleep all day. Most of them were much younger than me, so I remember how stupid I was at their age. It just made it very hard for someone detoxing. While I enjoyed the interaction with them at times, there were also times when I just needed some quiet, but that was a rare occurrence.

Of all the drugs that I reminisced about, cigarettes were the one thing that I craved every day. That was the one thing that wasn't illegal that I enjoyed, but smoking wasn't allowed in the jail anymore, so I had to hold out hopes that someone would sneak some tobacco in. Yes, the jail was supposed to be this super-secured facility, but the occasional contraband would surface from time to time.

The first time I got in on a few hits from a cigarette, I nearly threw up, just like the first time I had ever tried to inhale in my early teens. And the buzz was like, oh my word! Who knew that a few months without a cigarette would produce such a high as that? Maybe I was mistaking the dizziness from the cigarette as a buzz. Either way, it was worth the risk we were taking.

I can't remember the exact timeline for this, but one day, a detective from Powell County showed up at my unit, wanting to speak to me. They didn't put us in a private room or anything; they made me sit in the commons area where every inmate in the unit could see what was going on. Needless to say, you can imagine what was going through their minds. They thought that I was snitching on someone, so I naturally became a person to be concerned about among the inmates in the unit until I could clear things up later.

The detective told me that he was investigating a case in Powell County, and my name had come up, and he needed to ask me a few questions. He asked me how long I had been locked up there in Lexington and if I knew a girl named Teresa. Once I answered his questions, he told me she had recently accused me of rape. She told them that I showed up at her house one night and raped her. What she didn't know was that I had been locked up in the Lexington jail for several months, including the time when she said the rape occurred.

You talk about being glad you're locked up. That's the best alibi one could have. There's definitely no disputing that. I don't know the circumstances around what she may have been involved in, and why accuse me of rape? Perhaps it had something to do with the case the grand jury indicted her on and the fact that she must have thought I told them about something that caused them to reopen their investigation; I don't know. I hadn't been involved with her all summer, much less talked to her.

When it would come time for me to have another court date in Powell County, a sheriff's deputy would come to Lexington to get me the day before and take me up there for my court appearance. This happened multiple times over the remaining few months of my case there, and I liked getting out of the Fayette County jail for a little change of atmosphere. The most exciting part for me was that I could smoke while away from Lexington. Powell County still allowed prisoners to smoke, so that was something that I would look forward to. After my court appearance, they would bring me back to Lexington the next day.

Chapter XXII

The Road to Recovery

The first step to recovery for me was to seek forgiveness from God and my family, whom I had deceived for so long. It turned out that this would be the easy part. The hardest part was forgiving myself for all the pain I had caused others and the path of destruction I had left along the way. No matter how hard I tried to convince myself that there was nothing I could do but pray and leave it in God's hands, it was still an obstacle that would take some time for me to overcome.

The chemical part of the withdrawals was wearing off, and my body was still getting used to living without the addictive substance daily. However, the mental mindset was proving to be more of a struggle for me. I had always been more comfortable retreating to my comfort zone when I needed to be alone, but this wasn't an option.

Day after day, night after night, spent in this environment, was taking its toll on me emotionally. There was so much concrete and glass for the constant noise to bounce off at all hours of the day and night; it seemed never-ending. I just wanted to explode with rage at times, but I had seen where that had gotten anyone who tried it, and I wasn't looking for trouble.

To keep my mind occupied on something other than the constant noise, I would close my eyes and try to remember the words of some of the hymns we sang in church while growing up. At first, I could remember a few bits and pieces of some of the more familiar hymns, and over time, I began to remember more of the verses and even some of the other songs.

This helped calm me when I felt overwhelmed, and it became a routine for me each night to help me fall asleep. Each night before falling asleep, I asked God to give me a song to help bring me some much-needed comfort, and I often woke the next morning with a song in my head.

Eventually, those checks that I had written were starting to come back to haunt me. I guess the incident with my arrest sparked an investigation into the account on which the check was written. I discovered that the account number associated with the old check from my dad's business was now a new account number for a different bank and person. It turned out that the account now associated with the number was a lady who apparently didn't keep up with her account very often and had no idea of the money being deducted from her account.

One by one, those checks started making their way through the system, and every time one would surface, new charges were being handed down to me. Each time a new charge was entered, I would be taken back down to booking and rebooked on each count, fingerprinted, and returned to my cell. This went on for every check I had written. I don't remember exactly how many there were, but it was somewhere in the ballpark of seventeen checks. That's seventeen new felony possession of a forged instrument charges tacked on to the original charges.

Every time I had a court appearance, they would round everyone up, take us down to the intake area, and place us in a small cell until it was time to leave. The jail was miles from the courthouse, so we had to be bussed to court each time. When it was time to load the buses, they would line us all up in the hallway alongside a long chain lying on the floor. Attached to that chain every few feet were shackles, which are basically handcuffs for the ankles. If you've never tried to walk with shackles, try chaining your feet together with a piece of chain about three feet long and then try walking.

We were then all handcuffed and led to the bus for the trip to the courthouse. It's very difficult to walk, but then you add the guards yelling to move faster (probably on purpose). It was impossible to move too fast. Otherwise, you would fall down, and if that happened, you would take someone else with you, and that wasn't pleasant, especially if the guy behind or in front of you was twice your size. The trips to the courthouse happened at least once, sometimes twice a month, depending on your case.

I couldn't wait for this to be over with. The reality that I was facing some prison time was obvious to me. With all of the new charges on top of the charges in Powell County, any hope of probation had now been thrown out the window. The best I could hope for at this point was some court-appointed drug rehabilitation, but there weren't as many facilities back then as there are today that offer in-house treatment. The likelihood that I was facing prison time was very real, and the thought of that scared the hell out of me to even try and process it.

It took a while for me to allow my parents to visit me while I was in Lexington. Visits were behind a thick sheet of glass, and you communicated with each other over the telephone. My sisters, Jackie and Glenda, took turns bringing Kelli by to see me, and that way, everyone got a chance to visit, but even that was hard to deal with. On the one hand, you are happy to see friendly and familiar faces, but on the other hand, it makes you miss them, even more, to see them face to face and then watch them as they leave. Often, I would leave first.

I also talked with my family by phone regularly, and they helped me with a little money for commissary items and phone calls while I was there, which meant everything to me. I would use the money to buy paper, envelopes, stamps, and some snack items. The commissary was like money in jail. If you had commissary items, you could trade them for other items, and it was always used to gamble with. Some even had what they called 'stores' of the commissary. You purchased on credit. One honeybun now in return for two when you get your items in.

Writing was something that kept my mind occupied, and it was a way for me to explain myself better than on an emotional phone call that everyone in the pod could hear. As loud as it was in there, it made phone conversations difficult. I had to talk loud because of all the noise, and I couldn't talk about my feelings without getting very emotional, so writing became the silent escape. I tried to convey my apologies for all of the stupid stuff I had done, but those words didn't have much meaning at first. My family had heard it so many times before and then watched as I continued my destructive lifestyle.

For me, it was therapy, and I needed to say what I said and hope that someday I could begin to repair all that I had destroyed. It turned out that my momma, God bless her soul, saved every one of the letters and drawings I had sent her while I was locked up. The envelopes and pages within were almost always covered with artwork. We all did it to pass the time and make the letters have as much meaning to the reader as possible.

Mom wrote to me every single week while I was incarcerated. I don't think she ever missed a week. She would even put the week number at the top of the page, representing how many weeks I had been gone. I was her baby, and I could do no wrong in her eyes. It broke my heart to think I had hurt her as I did. She always told me that she was praying for me and that someday, God would bring me back home to her.

My oldest sister, Glenda, spoke to me several times about the minister at the church she was attending and told me about his journey with addiction. He had spent a little time in federal prison, so I asked if she could get me his name and address so I could write to him sometime. Once I got his address, I wrote to him and asked him to come and visit me sometime, and he did not long after he received my letter. It was a great visit; he was such a genuine person who assured me I would come through this just fine. He prayed for me and told me that if I ever needed anything, please get in touch with him. I left the visit that day feeling much better.

I was raised to believe that God was always present, but I sure didn't feel like that was the case with me. I hadn't felt His presence in my life for a long time, and I knew why. It's not that God had left me because of the lifestyle I was living. In fact, He was there the entire time. It was me that wasn't present. Matthew 7:7 says, "*Ask and it will be given to you; seek and you will find; knock and the door will be opened to you.*"

The problem was, I wasn't seeking Him. I had chosen a path other than what I had chosen as a teenage boy, which was in the opposite direction. I didn't want God in my life. The path I chose didn't include God because I had tried that path and thought my way was the better road to take.

After traveling that path for over twenty-five years, I began to see how much I had screwed it up—divorce after divorce. Destructive lifestyle after destructive lifestyle and failure after failure had left me a very bitter and hard-hearted person. I had made a life of blaming everyone else for my failures and had never once accepted responsibility for the consequences of my actions. But how do you return from all of that? How do you forget everything and just walk away a better person? In my mind, that wasn't possible. I couldn't even sleep at night without the nightmares that wouldn't go away. It constantly reminded me of my failure in every aspect of my life.

I once had a beautiful home that I built with two hands. Opportunity after opportunity to make a great family structure and two great kids that could have had the best life a kid could ask for. But I never saw those as opportunities; I saw them as failures. With each one, I plunged the knife of self-destruction further and further into my soul until I cut off the lifeline that provided me with those opportunities. I pushed God away because I couldn't see Him as the provider, only the one I kept failing. Why would He see me as anything other than who I truly was?

I was the woman at the well that day (John 4). Always seeking the things that could not satisfy. He knew my every sorrow, He saw my every tear, and He heard my every cry. Even in my darkest hour, He was there; I just didn't look for Him. I was too busy dealing with self-pity and failures to look for Him, knock, and ask. He didn't seem present because I failed to invite Him in, but He was definitely there all along.

I can remember a dream I had one night in jail. It was very vivid to me then and still very present in my mind. I don't think that I have ever shared this with anyone before. I didn't feel the need to because it wasn't a message for anyone other than me and me alone at that very moment.

I remembered as I was trying to fall asleep that night asking God for strength like Jesus had to face these fears that I was facing. I mean, for Jesus to know what His future held and to have been so strong to face it head-on without fear. That had to take a lot of strength and courage. I just wanted to understand what it was like not to fear the obvious consequences I was about to face. That's when I drifted off to sleep.

In my dream that night, I awoke in a wooded area. It was dark outside, and I was alone. I heard someone weeping. It sounded like a man's cries. As I looked beyond the wooded area just in the clearing beneath a tree, I saw a man weeping, face down in his arms. Then I woke up, and the first thought that entered my mind when I awoke was the garden of Gethsemane. I instantly recognized the man in my dream as Jesus. I remembered the story from my childhood about Jesus going to the garden to pray before His crucifixion. *Matthew 26: 36-46*

I always thought He was just Jesus. Cool, calm and collected Jesus. But He was begging His father not to make him do this unless it was His will. Twice he asked Him to take the cup from him. He was weeping because He was afraid. Why, then, should I be afraid? Just when I found myself seeking Him most, He was there, just as He always had been.

My eyes were opened to a whole different aspect of living that night. It was okay to be scared because the unknown is almost always uncomfortable. You have to find a way to overcome the fear with faith. You cannot allow fear to win. Jesus knew His future, and He was afraid, but He also trusted that His Father was in complete control and carried out the mission He was sent to Earth to do.

Nearly a year from the time that I was first arrested in Powell County, the case was closing in on a plea agreement offer from the prosecutor. In exchange for a guilty plea, they would recommend a five-year sentence. That was reasonable because I was facing as many as ten years for the charges there. I had asked if I could wait for final sentencing until my case from Lexington was complete in hopes of combining both sentences, but since they were in different counties, all they could do was ask the court to consider it.

My Lexington case was nearing its end as well. They offered to combine all of the forgery charges into one, dismiss the possession of drug paraphernalia and recommended a one-year sentence to run consecutively with my sentence from Powell County. A total of six years in the state penitentiary with credit for time served in both cases meant that I would have to serve a minimum of fourteen months in prison before I would be eligible for parole. There was no guarantee that I would be granted parole after that time, but at least there was the possibility, and for me, that was a sign of hope.

It would still be several weeks to a month before everything was finalized and I could be transported to the state's custody. I was ready to get the process started so I could start working on preparing for the parole board, but knowing that I would be leaving for prison soon brought on a whole new level of anxiety. All that I could picture in my head was the movie Shawshank Redemption. You know, the movie. It portrays prisoners in the worst of prison facilities, and the fight for survival among the prisoners regularly was all that I could picture in my mind.

Several guys in the Lexington jail had been to prison before, and most agreed that it was much better than jail. You had much more freedom to move around at the prison and more opportunities to get out each day and work or even sign up for educational classes like the GED program. I had never finished high school and never really needed a diploma. Still, the idea sounded appealing because it would allow me to accomplish something positive for a change and look good when I met with the parole board.

I had asked a million questions about what to expect, but nothing can prepare you for it until you experience it yourself. Even with first-hand knowledge, the reality is nothing like how you play through it in your mind. To say that I was terrified is a fair statement, but I knew that this would happen, and I had to find a way to wrap my head around it and keep myself together because the time to be a big boy had come.

Chapter XXII

The Fish Tank

I think it was around early to mid-February of 2004 when the night guard called for me to pack my things. I knew what this meant; it was time to go. No time left to be anxious about the future; just focus on right now. The night guard was still on duty because it was probably 4:00 AM when they called for me.

Everything that I had tried to prepare myself for during the last few months was now becoming a reality. I had watched as guys in our unit had left before, and now it was my turn. I knew that the number of things I could keep with me would be minimal, so I only gathered personal items like pictures, letters and my paperwork and waited for the guard to come and get me.

The process from there was a lot like when we went out for court, only this time, we were given orange jumpsuits and handcuffed using a somewhat different restraint system for prisoner transport. Your handcuffs were attached to a chain around your waist which was attached to the shackles around your ankles.

Only about a dozen of us were being transported that day, so once everyone had been processed, we were led out to a transport van waiting in the sally port. The only thing I knew for certain was that we were headed to the Roederer Correctional Complex Assessment Center, also called the "fish tank" in LaGrange, Kentucky. This is where all inmates convicted and sentenced to state custody are taken to be processed and assessed. From there, they are transported to the facility where they will serve their time.

Upon entering the LaGrange facility's entrance, the first building you see is the Kentucky State Reformatory. A huge stone building that looked like a castle, or even worse, the Shawshank Redemption. Yes, just like I had pictured it in my head in the months leading up to my arrival. Built in the 1940s, this place looked as wicked as anything in a movie, and I knew I would die there. Luckily, the van drove past it and around to the Assessment Center in the property's backside. There were actually three prisons on the grounds. Roederer, Kentucky State Reformatory and Luther Luckett Complex.

The assessment center is referred to as the "fish tank" because this is where every state inmate in Kentucky is brought for evaluation. Every level of the criminal, from child support to murder, was housed together. The only prisoners kept separate were those in protective custody, like sex offenders and state witnesses. Every inmate goes through the evaluation process based on their crime and sentence level; they are then assigned to specific prisons around the state to which they would eventually be sent.

The first order of business after arriving in LaGrange was a new hairstyle. Not much of a style, though; everyone got the exact same cut, buzzed! Guys who had been working on dreads for years were watching them hit the floor. No mercy. No facial hair either, only a small mustache if you wanted, but everything else had to go. Pretty humiliating if you ask me, but that was just the beginning!

The next stop in the intake system was the scrubbing and hose down. Yep, no dirty butts were getting through this nice clean facility, no sir! You are literally made to strip naked and stand in a line, side by side. The guard then came by with two spray bottles filled with no telling what and began spraying you down in your not-so-private-anymore areas and then told you to scrub down for thirty seconds, then step into the shower area and rinse off.

Then and only then were you issued clothes, bedding and hygiene items, then it was off to housing. After being processed and assigned to a bunk, I saw a familiar face. One of the guys in my pod from Lexington had been shipped out a few weeks before I was there. A little Hispanic dude that I called "Johnny." I called him that because he had so many aliases that even he didn't know his real name. It was good to see a familiar face and someone that had been there long enough to explain what to expect next.

Our unit was lined with 15 bunks down each wall. Sixty inmates of all kinds. Never in my life would I have imagined the many different kinds of people I saw there. Very young to very old, rough-looking to clean-cut, walking on their own to wheelchair bound. It became very clear early on that the law didn't discriminate. Everyone there had been convicted, but to hear them tell it, they were all innocent. I've never seen so many liars in one place in all my life. I accepted my guilt early on and didn't try to deny it.

Have you ever heard the saying, 'The dog with the loudest bark is the one most afraid'? That became very clear early on in my observations. Some of the biggest, meanest-looking guys were the loudest. Always barking off some kind of threats. I'm here to tell you that you better look out for the quiet little guy over in the corner. I started feeling sorry for them because they seemed to be easy targets for the big dogs, but even the smallest, quietest dog can be vicious when you back it into a corner and poke it enough.

As for the chow, it was remarkably much better than I had anticipated, especially when you compared it to the bland food I had been used to eating for the last several months. I would actually look forward to chow time. Initially, it was a little intimidating because they ran you through there faster than a Chick-Fil-A drive-through. They only had limited time to feed everyone, so there was no room for loitering around. I'll never forget the saying the COs would yell out constantly during chow; "Let's go! Eat it now; taste it later"! CO stood for Corrections Officer. It's what the inmates called them.

You only had enough time once you stepped outside to light up a smoke and get a few good drags before entering the chow hall, so you had to kill it, stick it behind your ear, and finish it off after chow on the way back to the unit. It didn't take long to get the routine down, and the weather was starting to get a little warmer each day, so when they let us out in the yard, it was a nice change of pace. I hadn't felt the warm sunshine on my face for a long time.

I distinctly remember the first day we were allowed to go to the yard. I sat on the walkway's edge, leaned back against the building facing the sun, closed my eyes and soaked it all in. For just a small moment in time, I was free with my eyes closed to my surroundings. I could picture myself on a beach somewhere soaking up the sunshine. For the first time in a very long time, my mind could relax and explore something calm for a change. The fresh air was good for the soul, and I took it in before opening my eyes and returning to reality.

The yard wasn't huge, but plenty enough space for some workout equipment, a few basketball courts and a walking path. I wasn't interested in the weight pile or basketball, so I walked around the path or sat at one of the picnic tables and enjoyed being outside. Spring is one of my most favorite times of the year, and I couldn't remember the last time I had just been outside and stopped long enough to enjoy the sunshine. The grim reminder of where you were was evident in the razor wire adorning the fences. You could see someone's farmland just beyond the property, so it was easy to let your imagination run wild if you let it.

I was at this facility for about six weeks while they did my assessment. Then I was moved over to the minimum-security area of the campus to the Substance Abuse Program building, where they housed the substance abuse inmates. I was hoping this would be my new home for a while because I wanted and even asked about getting into the program while I was incarcerated. Still, it turned out to be a holdover until a bed was available at the facility where I would be sent later.

The commissary items at this facility were awesome. Name-brand cigarettes and Little Debbie snacks of all kinds. I had a little money on my account, so I stocked up on goodies because I had heard that most other facilities didn't have these name-brand items available in their commissaries. It may be a while before I would indulge in this luxury.

For security purposes, they wouldn't tell us which facility we would be going to until the day and time of the transport. That's classified information, and we wouldn't know any of it until it happened. Until then, I just managed to adjust to my new way of life. Never really getting too comfortable because this was just temporary.

Chapter XXIII

The Gray Ghost

By now, it's probably mid-April of 2004, and the time had come to be shipped to my new facility. The anxiety level increases every time change happens, mostly due to the unknown nature of the situation, but it's not something that you have any say in the matter, so you have to put on the big boy pants and accept whatever it is that comes.

Once we were all packed up, including all the goodies, they walked us back to the intake area so we could be processed and prepared for transport. That meant back into the orange jumpsuits and chained up in the cuffs and shackles once again. Once everyone had been processed, they loaded us onto the gray ghost. That was the name of the big Greyhound bus specifically designed for prisoner transport—basically, a prison on wheels.

I remember that ride all too well, which is still very vivid in my mind today. We finally knew our destination, but it was not a place I had ever heard of, and I had no idea where it was located other than somewhere in the state of Kentucky. Marion County Correctional Complex was a minimum-security facility just outside Lebanon, Kentucky.

Because of security measures, the route was never the same when transporting prisoners, and almost never on an interstate. This meant we would travel the backroads through the countryside all the way there. Sounds pretty nice until you factor in that the seats in the bus were very smooth and slippery, so with every sharp curve along the country roads meant that you would slide from one side of the seat to the other. Your hands were cuffed to your waist in the front, so holding on wasn't much of an option; you just had to ride it out.

There were many prisoners on the bus that day being transported to various prisons around the state, and Marion County just so happened to be the first stop of the day, which I was very thankful for after the nearly two-hour slip-and-slide journey. By the time we arrived, I was worn out from trying to prevent myself from sliding right out onto the floor the entire trip. And besides, I sure could use one of those Little Debbie snack cakes right about then.

Upon arriving at the Marion County facility, we were bussed to the backside of the property, which was an Old Catholic college converted to a minimum-security prison facility. It looked like a nice place on the surface; at least the grounds weren't like your typical prison yard; it looked more like a college campus. Since it was a minimum-security facility, there wasn't all of the razor wire surrounding every inch of the property, which made it a little easier to cope with.

Once we were all unloaded and processed into the facility, we were issued our new khaki uniforms, essentials and bedrolls and told that we needed to walk back up to the main building at the very front of the property, where we would check in to medical for our evaluation. We took a good half-mile hike back through the property in the drizzling rain to the main building we went. We were told we had to be medically cleared before returning to get our stuff and head to our assigned cells. All of which, I might add, were located back up in the same building as medical.

A second trip in the drizzling rain, only this time, packing all of our belongings and bedroll. We only had a short window of time to get back to our cells before the afternoon count time when everything was locked down. I wasn't going to make it, so they had to come with the van, load my stuff up, and drive me back before lockdown. That was so exhausting, and all I could think about was those Little Debbie snacks. I was about to pig out heavy; at least, that was my plan.

Once I managed to drag everything up to the dorm's third floor and down to the very end of the building, literally the very last room at the end of the hall, I was beyond exhausted. I made it to my bunk just in time for the afternoon count time. It was mandatory for everyone to be in their cell, standing beside their bunk for the count. It was all I could do to stand there long enough without passing out until they finished counting. Once that was over, I was ready to settle in and tear into those Little Debbie snacks.

As I started unpacking my stuff, I realized someone had gone through my bag and taken every one of my Little Debbie snack cakes. Are you freaking kidding me? I was pissed! Apparently, when they unloaded our stuff from the bus, all of our personal items were left in the hallway unattended while we were getting cleared by medical and free game for anyone walking by. I was devastated! I had been thinking about those all day long.

There were a handful of inmates working up there in the intake area, helping unload the bus. Apparently, this was the ultimate job to have because anything and everything was fair game. "Welcome to prison" was the response from the CO when I told him what had happened. He probably had one of my Ho Ho's in his pocket. This was my new reality. I learned very early on to watch my stuff like a hawk, and complaining to the COs was useless. From then on, everything went in my locker, and the lock was kept locked even when I was in my cell.

After count time, I was able to meet the other five guys that shared the cell. Actually, it was a dorm room because, as I said before, this used to be a catholic college campus. My bunkmate said his name was Kenneth. He was a rather large, bulky African American dude who looked very intimidating, but the more we got to know each other, the more I realized what a teddy bear he was. He worked out a lot at the weight pile and spent the rest of his time working with the chaplain.

His routine was as regular as a clockwork. He would be up at the crack of dawn and in the breakfast chow line first thing. Then to the shower and off to the chapel to work. I noticed the Bible on the table beside his bunk when I arrived, so I knew he had to be a good guy.

During my time there, we connected like brothers. So much so that my mom started sending him birthday cards, and they eventually got to meet one day when we were both at a visitation at the same time. To this day, we still keep in touch. He's a special kind of friend you would never expect to meet in those circumstances, but I still consider him one of my best friends.

Chapter XXIV

Repairing The Damage

One of the first things I did after getting settled was to enroll in the GED program there. I had a lot of time to kill, and I couldn't think of a better way to spend it than by working to finally get a high school diploma after twenty-eight years. At first, it was a little intimidating, but I was surprised at how quickly some of the stuff came back to me after so long.

Math was the easiest because I had used it many times while working in construction. The other subjects started a little slower, but eventually, I began to catch on, and when it came time for the big test, I passed on the first try. For the first time in a very long time, I had accomplished something positive, and even though I didn't really need it at this point in my life, it felt good to achieve something I had worked so hard on.

The next thing that I wanted to work on was a newer pair of glasses. The ones I had been using were a very old prescription, and it was all I could do to see well enough to read and write. The state provided these services for free, but getting on the list to see the eye doctor and actually get started on ordering a pair proved to be a bit more challenging, but I had time to kill.

The same applied to the medical doctor. I experienced several episodes during my incarceration with the infected gallbladder. Even though I tried to explain it to them each time, I knew what it was because of my earlier diagnosis, they thought I was just another prisoner that knew everything, so they just treated me for acid reflux and sent me on my way.

I concluded that a lot of this discomfort was because you spend a lot of time laying in your bunk in prison, and I found that sitting up after meals was less painful and easier for my system to digest the food. Nevertheless, it was still an issue I would deal with for some time before I fell out of my bunk one afternoon and passed out from the pain.

I guess that was enough to prompt them to take me and have it checked out at the nearby hospital. It turned out that this time after they did an ultrasound, they determined that I had gallstones and that my gallbladder was seriously infected and about to burst. If that had happened, it could have easily killed me. After a few more doctor visits, they scheduled me for surgery to remove my gallbladder.

Step by step, I was beginning to piece my life back together. I was in a different state of mind now without all of the stimulants, and I could start repairing the damage I had caused along the way, both physically and mentally. The physical damage I had caused to my body over the years would, in some ways, not be repairable, like lung damage, but I could repair some of the things like dental work that needed to be repaired and restored in the worst way.

Dental service was also offered there in the prison system, and the state covered those procedures as well. Not the best dental professionals available, but I was able to get started on removing some of the infected and broken teeth that were giving me so much trouble. Eventually, they had to remove all of my upper teeth because those were the ones most damaged by the sinus issues caused by snorting so much over the years. I still had quite a few of my lower teeth, but many of those also had damage.

During a phone call home to the family one week, they informed me that my friend Owl had passed away. I hated to hear that news. I was hoping to have an opportunity to thank him in person for putting up with all of the crap that I brought into his life. He was always the jokester and always had something funny as hell to say, even if it was a stab at my sexual preference. I really hate that I wasn't able to speak with him again.

One of the biggest fears I had about being away from my family was the fear that one or both of my parents might not be around by the time I got home. When I heard about Owl's passing, which hit home for me in a real way, I begged God not to take them from me until I could hold them again. Many emotional things are very hard to deal with in prison, and the death of a family member or someone close is very hard to process.

Meanwhile, I had been keeping in touch with Whit, the pastor my sister mentioned when I was in the Lexington jail. I had asked him if he thought he could come to the prison sometime and give his testimony. I hadn't heard any more about it, so I just figured that the state wouldn't allow it, and I had pretty much given up on it happening when I heard from Whit one day, and he said he and a few members of the choir were going to be coming soon. That was awesome!

I had heard a little about his testimony from my sister but not the whole story, so I was looking forward to them coming. Kenneth helped promote it through the chaplain, and they had a really good response from the population. My sister would also be coming because she sang in the choir. The minister of music had put together some music that went along with the theme of the testimony, and the choir had been traveling around presenting it for some time. From what I had heard, it was a powerful testimony, and I was looking forward to it.

When the time came for the program, it was a packed house. Inmates soak up any opportunity to see new faces, and I think they enjoy listening to someone's story of redemption. It gives you a sense of hope. By the time the program had finished, you could feel a difference in the room. The presence of God was moving throughout that room that night. I don't remember how many decisions for Christ were made, but it was multiple, and that is what made it worth every minute of it.

Whit is a very genuine and passionate pastor, and I finally got a moment to speak to him that night without a glass wall between us. I told him that I was coming to that church and joining up with the choir once I was released. I wanted to be a part of that, and I would someday have a testimony to share. I managed to stay in touch with him over the next several months as he helped me understand some of the questions I had about recovery through mail correspondence.

Chapter XXV

Parole Hearing

My first chance to see the parole board was quickly approaching, and I was becoming increasingly terrified. I had seen countless numbers of guys get their hopes up because they had done everything the board recommended the last time they saw them, only to be denied once again. First-timers with non-violent charges had a better chance of making parole their first time up, but the anxiety leading up to the hearing date was terrifying. You don't want to appear overly confident because you may have to walk out of the hearing with disappointing news. You also don't want to come out of the hearing bouncing around like a kangaroo rubbing it into everyone else that has to stay.

In the weeks leading up to my hearing, I had been experiencing some very vivid dreams at night, and Kenneth and I would try to interpret them each day based on our biblical beliefs. Some are too complicated to explain, and some so personal that I don't need to explain, but very vivid nonetheless. Each one seemed to have a message or confirmation of something I had recently questioned. I was beginning to see that when I sought Him, He was there.

I want people to know that, for me, this was my experience and that it is not my belief that this is something that everyone has to experience. I questioned God many times during my incarceration, and I honestly believe that He sometimes uses dreams as an opportunity to communicate with us. Psalm 46:10 says, *"Be still and know that I am God."* I wasn't having conversations with Him, but He had a way of using dreams to reveal certain things.

For me, sleep had been a time of torture in the more recent past. The psychological warfare that had been going on in my head never seemed to stop. But now, I have noticed things are beginning to change in my thought pattern. This was a time of restoration for me, both mentally and physically. Although I would never have chosen this path, I recognized it as a time that was very necessary for me to repair myself from the inside out.

It was early October when the time finally came for me to see the parole board, and my anxiety level was off the chart. I had mentally prepared myself for the worst possible answer, but there was also the possibility that I could go home soon. All that I could do was go in there and be one hundred percent honest with them.

It's their job to listen to the stories from the inmates that have had plenty of time to conjure up, and I'm sure they have heard some good ones over the years. And for many of the inmates, this wasn't their first time before the board, so they have probably heard it all, and then some, time after time.

I didn't know how this process would go, but I did know that my sister Jackie would be attending the hearing on my behalf. She, of all people, knew me back and forth. She was the closest of my siblings in age, and she had dealt with me and my addictive lifestyle for many years. Most of the time, she wanted to choke me due to the lifestyle I had been living because she saw firsthand what it did to our parents emotionally.

But this time was different. She was one of my closest alibis and the one I confided in most often, so she knew the change that had taken place within my heart, and she was willing to testify on my behalf. It was also nerve-racking for her, but she showed up, and to me, it was a huge relief to have someone on my side.

She was the one that had been pre-approved as my home placement if I was granted an early release, and that meant that she would be charged with the task of keeping me in line and making sure that I reported when I was supposed to and followed through with any other recommendations that they might have as part of an early release. She was a former drill sergeant in the army, so I knew she had it in her to make me toe the line.

Once the hearing had taken place, we were both sent to wait in the hallway until they made their decision. I felt good about everything that had taken place, and I didn't go in making many promises because I knew that if I were granted an early release, my actions would speak for me from that point on. Failure to follow their recommendations or any new charges would be grounds for revoking my parole, and I would be sent back.

I had seen this time after time while in jail and throughout my stay in the state's custody. There were as many guys in there that had violated their parole and been sent back, or even worse, caught new charges while on parole than there were new inmates. I didn't want any part of that. If I am to get approved, I am walking the tightrope, and we all know what happens if you lose concentration and get off balance on the tightrope.

Once they had made their decision, they called me back into the room: just me and the board members. No family allowed. They began the longest possible explanation of what had taken place and reminded me of my charges and their seriousness. The time I had spent in custody so far, in their minds, was not nearly enough time for me to have rehabilitated my mind or long enough to satisfy the state that I had recovered from the lifestyle that I had become accustomed to for so long.

They did commend me on my accomplishments, like the GED that I had achieved, and just when I thought they were sending me back with a deferment, they told me they were taking a chance on me and granting me an early release. My heart sank. No, it dropped like a bomb in my chest and then to the floor. I wanted to scream! Then I wanted to cry, but I must remember where I was and maintain my composure.

I walked out of that room, trying my best to withhold the excitement, but their decision had to be obvious by the look on my face. My sister was still looking at me, waiting for the results, and she was as surprised as I was when I told her of their decision. I couldn't wait to tell everyone else, but I wouldn't know my actual release date for a few days. My sister and I decided that we would keep that information a secret. I didn't want my parents or Kelli to know what day I was coming home until I walked through the door.

The process usually took a few days before they would release me. Even though I heard it from their mouth, I wasn't allowing myself to get too excited because I had seen so many different times when someone would get as far as the gate only to be met by a deputy from another county or state waiting to take custody of them on an outstanding warrant. I was pretty positive that I didn't have any outstanding warrants anywhere, but you have to prepare yourself for the worst-case scenario, and I was on guard twenty-four-seven.

Chapter XXVI

Early Release

The thought of getting out terrified me to the core. On the one hand, you are excited to get out, but on the other hand, the unknown of where to even start is terrifying. I wanted to continue my sobriety once I was back out on the street, but I wasn't sure that I would be able to handle the pressure once I was released back out on my own. If I screwed it up, I would have the remainder of my six-year sentence hanging over my head.

I was paroling to my sister's house, which was comforting, but I knew she would hold my butt to the fire and make me walk straight and narrow. I would also have to complete six months of meetings that I would have to attend on a weekly basis and be subjected to random drug testing for the next five years. I didn't know if I could handle all of that.

I knew I wouldn't be able to return to Powell County because the parole board told me to stay away from there due to the charges I had received there. Still, my daughter lived there, so I would have to work out other arrangements with her mother to meet me halfway any time I wanted to get Kelli. To be honest, I didn't want to go back there. It was a dangerous place for me because of all that had transpired there over the last few years.

The only real friends I had all lived there, but they were also still involved in activities I could not be around if I were to maintain my sobriety. I had to make a whole new life for myself. One that included all new people adds a new level of anxiety to the mix. It's not like you just go to the store and shop for new friends. Where do I even start to build a whole new life? I was going to have to put my faith to the test on this one, but the stress level was building.

The time for my early release had finally come. I had received all of the necessary paperwork from my parole hearing, and all that was left to do was make it through just one more night. Nighttime had been a struggle for me for so long, but over time, I had been successful at keeping the routine of singing a hymn in my head to help me fall asleep, and this also seemed to prompt calmer thoughts for a more restful sleep pattern.

This night would be no different from any other night besides less sleep. After all, the next morning would be a day that I had looked forward to for such a very long time, and the anxiety had already been building for weeks. As I had done for so many months leading up to this night, I started my night with a simple prayer of thanks, but this night, a flurry of hymns drifted through my mind as I lay there trying to fall asleep. One in particular that I remembered was an old familiar hymn of invitation growing up that went like this…

All to Jesus, I surrender

All to Him I freely give,

I will ever love and trust Him

In His presence daily live.

I surrender all. I surrender all.

All to thee my blessed Savior,

I surrender all.

Just like a parent singing to a child at night in a soft, quiet voice. This would be my prayer tonight, and I would soon drift off to sleep.

It only seemed like a few minutes had passed since I drifted off to sleep when the CO came in, tapped on my bunk, and said it was time to go. When I opened my eyes and realized what day it was, I sat straight up in bed, trying to force myself to wake up. As I sat on the edge of the bunk, the melody of a song played through my head. It wasn't anything unnatural by this time because it happened quite often, only this time, something seemed so very different.

Like someone tickling the highest notes of the piano keys. Each note, one by one, very softly. It was familiar to me, but it was just a melody playing in my head at that moment. My mind was so full of emotions at that point, but as the song continued to play through my mind, I could almost feel the rush of demons being sucked from deep within my very soul. It was as if memory after memory of every troubled time was circling me in visions as it was drawn from me. The voices that had cried out to me so many times, reminding me of all the times I'd tried and failed, were being conquered and crushed by the voice of truth.

All the while, the soft sound of the melody kept playing in my head. Still in a daze, suddenly, I felt another tap on my bunk. The CO said, "We need to go." I looked up at him, and just then, the melody became very clear, and I began to sing the words to the song in my head...

"Blessed assurance, Jesus is mine.

Oh, what a foretaste of glory divine".

With each line I would sing, visions of those words became very vivid and real to me. What I was witnessing was a little taste of Divine glory.

You're an heir of salvation.

You're purchased of God.

You're born of His spirit.

You're washed in His blood.

And then, as I reached the chorus of that song, a flood of peace washed over me as I had never felt, and I began to weep...

This is my story;

This is my song,

Praising my Savior all day long.

A peace like never before washed over me at that very moment. I didn't understand it, nor did I even try to right then, but I somehow knew in my spirit that I had been fully redeemed. I knew that no matter what I faced from that day forward that I was going to be ok. I knew without a doubt that I had been set free, and as it says in John 8:36, *"If the Son sets you free, you will be free indeed."*

Addiction had been conquered. Grace had been given. I had been set free.

I would walk away from there that day, proclaiming my freedom from addiction. Never again would I refer to myself as an addict. Did I still have an addictive personality? Of course. That's human nature, but I would no longer refer to myself as an addict again.

Twenty-five years had passed since I first asked God for a story to tell, and even though I hadn't thought about that for many, many years, right then and there, my story was revealed to me through the song I had prayed for. One by one, pieces of the puzzle began to fall into place as confirmation of my faith. It's a puzzle that is still being assembled every single day of my life.

You could see it on my face and hear it in my voice that day. I had no idea what direction my life would go from that day forward, but I did know in my spirit that my faith had set me free, and my faith would be the wind beneath my wings that would carry me through the remainder of my journey called life.

You'd think that this would be the end of my story, but in fact, it's only just the beginning. It is, however, the end of my life as an addict. I had made my way through the twelve-step program while incarcerated, but now it was time for me to take the thirteenth step. For me, the thirteenth step was accepting the fact that I had been redeemed, and it was time to leave that lifestyle at the foot of the cross and walk away

Chapter XXVII

Invitation

If you are reading this book and struggling with addiction, whether it is drugs or alcohol, adultery or pornography, gambling or an eating disorder, whatever it is that you struggle with, whatever it is that has control of you, I am asking you right now, right where you are while reading, to stop everything and listen to me.

No matter what you are struggling with, what pulls you down, how many times you have been told that you are not good enough, somewhere, someone right now is praying for you: a parent, a grandparent, a sibling, a friend, or even me. Someone is praying on your behalf.

I want you to know that you can be set free from it. You don't have to wait until you get your life all together. Stop telling yourself that it won't ever happen to you. You're never too far down the road that you can't turn around and walk away from it. Lay it all at the foot of the cross and walk away.

I stand in agreement with you right now, and Matthew 18:20 says, *"When two or more are gathered in my name, I am there with them"*.

If you've never given your heart to Christ, recite this prayer with me…

"Dear God, I know I'm a sinner, and I ask for your forgiveness.

I believe Jesus Christ is Your Son. I believe that He died

for my sin and that you raised Him to life.

I want to trust Him as my Savior and follow Him as Lord,

from this day forward. Guide my life and help me to do your will.

I pray this in the name of Jesus. Amen."

This simple prayer is all it takes. If you truly feel in your heart that you have recited this simple prayer and meant every word, you have been saved. The rest of your journey starts today. God bless you.

If you are a Christian struggling with addiction, pray this prayer with me…

"God, You alone possess the power to break the chains of my addiction. Release me from the bondage of my addiction. Return me to my family and friends. Restore what has been stolen. I do not possess the strength alone, but through Jesus, I can do anything. Give me the strength to say no and turn my eyes to You.

Wipe away the fog in my mind and let me see clearly the deception of the enemy. He comes only to kill and destroy. Give me the vision to see who I am in You. Let nothing but a clear vision of who I am to You and the knowledge of your love satisfy any desire.

God, I need your help. I cannot stop this desire on my own. I need your strength. You promise to forgive sins through Jesus. Forgive me of the things I have done, said, and thought under the spell of addiction. Forgive me of my sins that led me to stray away from Your way and go my own way. Father, pull me from this pit and place my feet on the right way, the path that leads to you.

Thank you, Father, for protecting me from mortal harm. Thank you for the grace that brought me to this place, seeking you. Thank you for the healing to come. Thank you that you are a Father of second chances, giving grace when it is needed most. Thank you for hearing my prayers. In Jesus' name, Amen."

In the back of this book, you will find a space to write your first name and the date you prayed if you have said either of these prayers. Just a first name and date will suffice. Then I want you to look at the other names that might already be there and pray for them. After that, pass this book on to someone else you know who is struggling. Everyone reading this book will see your name and pray for your continued strength.

If you are a parent, grandparent, sibling, or friend of someone who is bound by addiction, I hear your cry. I do not want you ever to give up praying for that loved one. Pray for the chains to be broken, lives to be restored, and for physical and mental healing to occur. When you pray, do so with conviction that it has already been answered. If you have to go somewhere and cry out loud to the heavens on their behalf, then do so right now.

Chapter XXVIII

Re-Entry

Ironically enough, my release date was October 21, 2004, my daughter's thirteenth birthday. I couldn't think of a better birthday present than her father coming home a changed man. She knew that I had seen the parole board and that I would be coming home at some point, she didn't know it was that day, and neither did my parents because I wanted to surprise all of them. Only my sister and Micki knew, and they were the ones that came to pick me up that day.

They had been parked outside the gate since very early that morning because they didn't want to take the chance of me getting released and not having someone there to pick me up. I still remember that day like it was yesterday. Kenny had met me at the front because he didn't want me to leave without a chance to say goodbye. We had built a special bond during our time together as bunkies, and I was looking forward to seeing him again on the outside someday.

The only clothes I had were prison issues and sweatpants, and I wasn't about to wear those anywhere, so my sister brought me some pants and a shirt to change into before heading home. As we drove out and through the guard shack, I thought there was still the chance that the guard would notice something on my paperwork and take me back into custody. You try to be prepared for anything, but he looked it over, smiled and said congratulations and be safe. Every turning point of that trip was overwhelming.

We stopped at a convenience store so I could get a real pack of cigarettes and a lighter. I hadn't used a lighter in nearly two years. It was the smallest of things that seemed huge to me now. I was apprehensive about going into the store because it felt like I wasn't supposed to be there. Your brain is trained to think a certain way in prison, and when you're suddenly removed from that atmosphere, your thought pattern is not quickly or easily reversed.

Even the smell on the outside was so very different. Everywhere that I looked, there was something different. I saw the world from a different perspective than I had in many years. I was just trying to take it all in and absorb it. I never wanted to forget what that moment felt like.

I remember pulling into my parent's driveway that day. The excitement had been building up the whole trip there, and now we were finally there. I wanted to surprise them, but I knew that my mom had heart issues, and the last thing I wanted to do was cause her to have a heart attack. They expected my sister to stop by, but neither knew I was with them.

Dad met them at the kitchen door, and he saw me first, but he was so caught off guard that he couldn't speak, and I held my finger to my lips as if to say; be quiet. Mom was seated at the kitchen table as she always was most mornings, and when I walked in behind my sister and saw me, she began to weep. Her emotions were impossible to contain, and it was all I could do to keep from losing it myself. There were no words. None were needed. Just hugs, lots of hugs.

These two prayed for me my whole life, especially every day while I was locked up, and Mom made a point to write to me every week, even if it was just a postcard, to let me know she was thinking about me.

I only had a limited amount of time before I had to report to probation and parole, but I really wanted to surprise my daughter for her birthday, so my sister drove me to her house. My sister told her I planned to call her for her birthday that afternoon so she would be sure and be at home when we arrived.

When we pulled up in the driveway, I expected her to come running outside to greet everyone, but no one came out, so the element of surprise was still on the table. We made our way to the front porch and knocked on the door. Kelli's aunt came to the door and called for her to come out. She came to the door with the house phone in hand, expecting a call from me, but when she saw me, she was stunned. She thought they had just let me out for her birthday, but I told her I was home for good, and you couldn't have slapped the smile off her face.

We didn't stay very long because we needed to get back to Lexington and check in with my parole officer, so after we had visited for a while, we headed back to Lexington.

Chapter XXIX

Parole

Once we returned to Lexington, I called to check in with probation and parole and was told to report first the next morning. My driver's license had expired while I was locked up, so I had to get my sister to take me and drop me off at the parole office the next morning. I wanted to be early because I didn't want to take any chances, and when I arrived, the doors were still locked, and quite a few people were standing out front on the sidewalk.

The crowd's demeanor soon clouded the exhilaration of being out of prison gathered outside. It was all criminals reporting to their officers, but just being in the crowd reminded me of being in jail. There's not a guilty party in the crowd. To hear them tell it, they were minding their own business and falsely accused, and they had no business being there. The funny thing is, you didn't see any business people standing there in the crowd, just criminals, and I was one of them.

I accepted my fate a long time ago. Even though I hated standing there amongst the early morning crowd, I knew it was necessary. I didn't want to be associated with them, but I also didn't want to be sent back to prison. So, as I had done many times before, I swallowed my pride and did what I had to do.

It seemed like an eternity for them to unlock the doors and let us in. Then, once inside, it took forever for me to be called upstairs to see my parole officer. It was like waiting at a doctor's office, where they make you sit and wait for what feels like an eternity before being seen. Finally, they called me up.

One thing that you come prepared to do each time, and that is being drug tested. Nothing is worse than peeking in a cup while someone stands and watches. I had been through this multiple times in prison, so it was nothing new. When I was called upon in prison to come to supply a sample, it never failed; I had just gone to the bathroom, and forcing a sample just wasn't an option when you get stage fright.

So, now that I am on the outside and know that I will most likely be tested when I get there, I don't want to take any chances, so I made sure not to go before I left the house just in case. I am waiting for my name to be called and about to pee in my pants. Sure enough, once I got upstairs to see my officer, he greeted me at the door with a cup and asked me if I would be clean. Not only will I be clean, but if we don't hurry, I will have a mess to clean up in the hallway!

They test the sample right then and there for multiple drugs like marijuana, cocaine, opioids and alcohol. You go straight into handcuffs and back to prison if you are dirty. I knew I wouldn't be dirty, but the anxiety was always present. My parole officer was the largest African American guy you'd ever seen. Very intimidating, to say the least. I remembered him as the one who came to the Lexington jail and did my PSI (pre-sentencing investigation).

Once he had gone through all of my release requirements and the third degree about what would happen if I ever broke the rules, he sent me on my merry way. I was glad that was over, but I would have to report every week for the next few months while I was settling in. That's when you are the most vulnerable. If you're going to repeat, catch new charges or fail to report, it would probably be during the first six months.

As part of my release, I had to report to what they called drug class once a week for the first six months. It was a lot like the AA and NA classes I attended while in prison. Nobody wanted to be there. Everyone in attendance was required to be there as part of probation or parole and to say this was helpful for recovery in any way, shape or form was a load of crap. It was a government-run facility just going through the motions so someone could collect a check. The biggest waste of time I had ever spent, but I showed up every week just as I was told for six months straight.

Parole was always there, looming over my head, waiting for me to screw up. I wasn't going back, at least not as a prisoner. One of the things I was very passionate about when I returned home was getting involved in a prison ministry somewhere. I had seen some evangelists on TV while incarcerated and wanted to get involved somewhere.

I was still on fire when I was released about sharing my story, but some obstacles would prevent me from doing things, such as going to jail to share my story because of my current status as a parolee. Nevertheless, I would continue to pursue every opportunity to get involved and do what I could.

I used this time to sit down and begin writing my testimony. I quickly found that order to put down what I had experienced into words meant that I would have to relive a lot of it, and that became very emotional for me. It would take me a year to complete the first version, and even with that, I hadn't even touched on any of the in-depth details of my journey because it consisted of forty-five years of my life.

Then, the dream of someday taking the time to sit down and write a more in-depth view of my journey would start. The condensed version of my journey that I used as a testimony, in the beginning was emotional enough, and that took me a year to complete, so the thought of a book was overwhelming and would take a back seat in my mind for twenty years.

Chapter XXX

Starting From Scratch

Soon after my release, my sister, Glenda, invited me to attend church and lunch afterward. I was really looking forward to going to that church, but I still wasn't comfortable being in public places with many people. As I said before, this is a real struggle for someone that has spent time away from the public. It was common for the anxiety to kick in at the thought of being out in public places, but I knew that I wanted to be a part of that church, and I trusted that God was in control and went anyway.

It was awesome that day. People I had never met before came up to me and told me they had been praying for me and were so glad to finally meet me. My sister had shared my story with her small group, and some of the choir members already knew my story from when they visited the prison with Whit to share his testimony. I felt more welcomed there than at church in a very long time. I couldn't wait to get back the following week.

After church, my sister asked me where I wanted to go for lunch. I didn't know what was around the area or what was a good place, so she recommended going to the Backyard Burgers in the nearby shopping center. I agreed that it sounded like a good place, and we headed that way. Once we had ordered our food and found a seat, I saw a familiar guy sitting across the room from us, having lunch with his family.

As we were eating our lunch, I kept looking over at that family, trying to figure out where I may know him from, and then it hit me. He was my second wife, Laurie's uncle Norman. After we finished eating, I got up, went to their table, and asked if he remembered who I was. They remembered me, and the conversation of his son immediately came up. He said his son was in the process of building a new house, and he needed a trim carpenter. I told him that I was fresh out of prison and didn't have the tools to do the job, but he insisted that his son had all the tools needed; he just needed an experienced carpenter to take on the job.

I told him that I was interested in talking to him, and we exchanged phone numbers, and he said he would have his son call me. I didn't think I would hear from him, though, and I was worried that even if he did call, would I still have what it took to take on a job like that right out of prison and years away from that type of work? Even still, there was a glimmer of hope that I had possibly found an opportunity for some work.

Jobs were not easy for someone with a felony conviction on their record, and even though I had been to many places filling out job applications, I still had to check that box on the application. I hated it because they never asked any questions beyond that point. Nobody cared whether or not I had cleaned my life up and was trying to do better; they just saw that as a red flag and assumed the worst from there. Even if I offered them a little insight into my current situation, they didn't care. It was their policy not to hire someone with a felony conviction. A policy that I feel needs to be re-written.

Society says that you are sent to prison to be rehabilitated. Still, when you are released and try to start over, they quickly forget about rehabilitation and play the felony card on you. The system doesn't want you rehabilitated because they don't make any money if you are reformed and can continue through life as a normal human being.

The next day, I got a call from Norman's son, little Norman, as most of the family called him. We talked for a while, and I explained to him my current situation, which he assured me didn't matter; he just needed a good trim carpenter to help with his house, and he trusted that I was the guy for the job. I agreed to meet with him the next day over at the house and look at what was involved, and then I could give him my decision.

Upon arriving at his house, I was blown away by the size of this place. I didn't know what this kid was doing to make money for a house that size, but as long as he wasn't a drug dealer, I didn't care. He had all the tools I would need; add that to the small collection of personal tools I could put together, and I was set for success. The drywall was almost complete, so we settled on a start date and hourly wage, and I couldn't thank him enough for the opportunity he was providing me with.

Had I not gone to lunch with my sister after church that day, this opportunity would not have been possible. I was convinced after that day that God provides us with the opportunities we need to succeed, and it is our place to be observant and make ourselves available to receive them.

I could have very easily declined the invitation to church and lunch that day because I wasn't sure if I was ready for it, but looking back on that day, I can see how it was lined up for me before I even knew it. From that day on, I have tried to see every invitation as a stepping stone of opportunity to move forward in my journey.

Chapter XXXI

New Life; New Things

With this new life, new things began to emerge. New opportunities were made available, and I spent most of my free time volunteering at my church, working in the media booth on the weekends, helping to create the graphics for the services and then working in the media booth most weekends. As well as volunteering with the media, I was interested in joining the choir. Still, singing wasn't easy without any teeth, so I began to seek out opportunities that would allow me to get some dentures made.

I eventually was able to find a dentist that worked with me on payments and was able to get some much-needed dental work done. The new smile was life-changing for me. I had been so self-conscious about my teeth for a long time and became withdrawn until I got some help, which turned everything around. I was able to smile again without shame. You probably have no idea what something so small can do for someone unless you've experienced it.

Now that I had a new smile, I did exactly what I said I would do and joined that choir. It was a small move that was just right for me. It allowed me to leave the house and become more social instead of sitting around. It was also a good opportunity to meet some new people.

I remember going with the choir to Eastern Kentucky with Whit as he shared his testimony, and I realized just before the concert that night that it had been one year to the day that Whit and some of the choir had come to the prison where I was at and shared his testimony. I reminded him of what I had told him that night when they visited the prison that someday I would be a part of that choir, and here we were.

One by one, things began falling into place in my life. Each time my faith confirmed that I was on the right path. I allowed God to direct my steps now instead of doing everything my way. I once heard a quote: "You can't walk on water if you're not willing to get out of the boat". I wasn't walking on the water but wasn't sinking either. I was focused on God, and with each step I took, I did so with complete trust in Him.

Another opportunity that I was involved in with the church was small groups. Our congregation was fairly large, and we had Saturday evening and two Sunday morning services, so unless you were involved in something like the choir or media, you didn't see anyone other than the people at the service you attended.

Small groups were way out of my comfort zone because they were much smaller than I had been involved with up until now. The first time I went to a small group, I drove around the block several times, even sat in the car out in front of the house long enough to chicken out, and went back home. I wasn't comfortable walking into someone's house I didn't know by myself, and my anxiety level was off the charts.

The next week, I drove there again, but this time, I mustered the strength act go in. As awkward as it was, it was equally as fun. Everyone was so friendly and welcoming. I left there that night with confirmation that God will take care of the rest when you take the first step.

After living at my sister's house for about a year, she sat me down one day and told me she thought the time was right for me to begin looking for a place to live independently. I tried my best to fight the thought of it, but at the same time, I knew that it was a necessary step for me if I were to learn how to manage life on my own again someday. We began looking into some options for small studio apartments that were affordable.

The whole time that I had been living with them, she had been helping me learn to manage my money and put away some from each paycheck to have when it came time to cover the bills each month, as well as a little cushion in the tough times when work might not be so plentiful.

I was still working on my own trimming little Norman's house. It took about a whole year to complete the job because he kept adding more work for me as time passed. That was a great opportunity because it paid good money and was dependable work.

Just as with job hunting, I quickly learned that renters were no different when it came to that one question on the application. I knew this would be the case, but what else should a person do? My parole officer is applying pressure on me to find my place, and frankly, I would love to have that opportunity, but my options needed to be better by this point. Each day, after apartment hunting, I would come home feeling defeated. It seemed as if no matter how hard I tried to do the right thing to get my life back on the right track, more doors were getting slammed in my face.

Chapter XXXII

Boy, You'll Never Win

By this time, I was getting pretty frustrated with God. How was I supposed to do the right thing when so many were against me? I was reminded of a song that was popular during that time from Casting Crowns called The Voice of Truth. One of the verses in the song says, "The giants calling out my name and he laughs at me. Reminding me of all the times I've tried before and failed. The giant keeps on telling me time and time again; Boy, you'll never win".

This is exactly how I felt. Society is the giant calling out my name and laughing at me. Reminding me repeatedly with each slamming door of all the times I've tried and failed and telling me that I will never win. So very frustrating, and it's beginning to take the wind from my sails, making it harder and harder to move forward in a positive direction.

Just when I was about to throw in the towel and give up on finding a place, I was reminded of the rest of that song. "The voice of truth tells me a different story. The voice of truth says, do not be afraid; this is for My glory. Of all the voices calling out to me, I will choose to listen and believe the voice of truth".

When faced with difficult times, human nature calls out "why"? And this is exactly what I was asking God. Why can't I catch a break when I am trying so hard to do the right thing? Why can't anyone see that I have changed and want to do the right thing? I never once thought to ask how. God, how can I do this? Show me the way, and allow me to see your direction.

There were still two more places on my list to stop by and put in an application. The first stop that day seemed decent. It was fairly newly renovated, and the price was in my range. When I sat down with them to review my application, I was amazed that even though they were concerned about my convictions, they said yes. I had finally found someone to give me a chance, but for whatever reason, when I left that day, I didn't feel right deep down.

I had one more place to see before calling it a day, and it was just across the road from this last place, so I stopped by the front office and filled out an application. While the manager was reviewing my application, one of the guys took me on a tour of the facilities. This was a nice place. They had a courtyard with a pool and an on-site laundry mat. The one-bedroom studio apartment we looked at was nice too, and I felt really good about this place.

After the tour, we returned to the office, and I sat with the manager to review my application. She told me immediately that it was not their policy to rent to someone with a felony conviction. I already knew that this would be their response, and I had even thought about not checking that box on the application to see if they did a background check, but I didn't do that. I wanted to get a place without having to lie about it.

After going back to my sister's house and thinking about it, I returned to the place that accepted my application, gave them the deposit, and finished the paperwork. When I arrived, I didn't feel good about the activity going down in the parking lot and between two buildings in plain sight of the office. I'd been around this kind of activity enough to realize what was happening, and I couldn't go through with taking that place.

By now, I was so frustrated. I finally found a place that would take a chance with me, and it turned out to be something I knew would drag me back down again. The second place I went to the day before was across the road, so I drove back there. Armed with the tenacity of a warrior refusing to be defeated, I returned to the office and asked to speak with the manager again.

I told her that I understood it wasn't their policy to lease to someone with a felony on their record, but I told her that she never asked me when that was or if I had even changed that lifestyle. I told her that I almost lied on the application and would take my chances on whether or not they would do a background check because I needed a place just that badly. I also told her of my will to turn that history into a positive ending, but I needed someone to believe in me. She told me that she would have to speak to her boss and then she would give me a call back as soon as she heard back from him.

Later that day, she called me and said that if I could get someone with a clean background to sign on my behalf, they would give me a chance. Wow! I had to talk my sister into signing for me, and I would have my own place. That wouldn't prove to be that easy, though. Even though my sister was the one helping me to get back on my feet, she was also the easiest to say yes to me, so she told me to ask Micki, her partner if she would sign for me.

Micki was the one that wasn't afraid to hold my butt to the fire. She told me right up front that this was her name at stake, and if I screwed it up as I had for so many others in the past, she was coming for me. She was also one of my biggest supporters and believed in me one hundred percent, and she agreed to go with me to sign the papers. This was a huge turning point for me. I was beginning to see more of the pieces to the puzzle fall into place.

My parole officer was equally happy to see that I had my own place now, but he always seemed to think I would eventually screw up and return to prison before my parole ended. He was accustomed to seeing it in most people, but he had never dealt with someone as desperate as I was to stay the course and make a new life for themselves. I was out to prove him wrong and wasn't afraid to tell him he was.

At that time, the recidivism rate for criminals that had been released was nearly forty-four percent within the first year of their release, and seventy-six percent returned within five years. I was determined not to be one of those statistics, and I had already made it past the first year, but I still had a way to complete the nearly five years I had on the shelf.

Chapter XXXIII

Prison Ministry

During my incarceration, I read a book called "Prison to Praise" and followed several television evangelists involved in prison ministries. This was something that I could get behind. I set my sights on jail and prison ministries and had high hopes of someday becoming involved in something like that once I was released.

It just so happened that the church I was attending had a prison ministry. The pastor was an ex-con, so why wouldn't they have a prison ministry? I spoke to the pastor, who gave me the name of the guy in charge. His name was George. I think he was one of the elders at the church at the time. He wasn't your typical prison ministry-looking guy, just a normal, kind-hearted soul with a passion for those less fortunate.

When I first hooked up with George, he was a little overwhelmed with all the ideas I was throwing out there. I was fresh out and on fire for blowing this ministry wide open, and he was just settled into his usual routine of visiting once a month and holding services at a nearby facility. He and maybe one other person was heading up the ministry, and I asked if we could meet and invite others interested to join us.

Our first meeting had a great turnout, and it snowballed from there. In my research leading up to this meeting, I learned of a national prison ministry called the Bill Glass Ministries. They traveled all over the United States, entering various prisons and holding all-day events for the prisoners. The best part I found when researching was that they had plans to come to Kentucky for an upcoming event.

I contacted them and filled out an application to become a team member. My problem was that I was still on parole, and it's a general rule of thumb that, as a felon, you are not allowed to associate with other felons. When I told the BGM about my current situation, they contacted me and told me that if I went in with their group, I could go. I immediately contacted my parole officer and asked him if I could go. Initially, he was a little apprehensive but reluctantly agreed to allow me to go in with them.

It just so happened that the prison where this event was to take place was the Roederer Correctional Complex (The Fish Tank), where I had spent the first couple of months of my sentence. The emotions I was experiencing were off the charts. I was so passionate about going in, but on the other hand, I was freaking out at the thought of being behind the fence again. Even if I were guaranteed to return home, I was still anxious about going in, but I felt a strong calling to go, and I was going no matter what.

Several people from our church signed up to go, as well as people from various other churches in the area. The BGM gathers local people in the event area and trains them on what to do and what not to do while there. They usually have some big sports names attend the event as a draw to the prisoners, and the event we were attending was well-known wrestlers on the circuit.

When the day finally came for the event, we were told to arrive bright and early and meet up in the parking lot. You can imagine my anxiety when we entered the facility that morning. It was too late to return, but I just wanted to throw up. I knew what to expect regarding the facility, but most group members had never experienced this.

We were taken in through the very exit I left from the day I was shipped out to the Marion County facility. One by one, we were escorted through the metal detector and into a holding area. When that gate closed behind us, a flood of emotions overcame me. I had heard that sound before. It's a sound you never forget, but it meant so much more to me this time. I was there for a different reason this time, and I had work to do.

We were escorted down the hall to a room where we would wait for the count to finish, and then we could head out to the yard. Everything about that place was still very familiar to me, from the smell to the noises of the inmates. I even recognized a few of the COs that were on shift that day. It was as if I had stepped back in time and relived this experience differently. The bell rang, which meant the count was clear, and it was time for us to head out to the yard.

We started the day involving the inmates out in the yard to draw the attention of as many inmates as possible. The morning yard time was all about connecting with the inmates, and then we all went to the chow hall and had lunch with them. After that, we returned to the yard for some more entertainment. Aside from the professional wrestler, there was a comedian that performed as well.

Now that they had the inmates' attention, they would begin to lead into their testimonies. Big, tough, muscular guys told of how hardcore they once were, some even had spent time in prison, and then they told of how God had transformed their lives and turned them around. They then told the volunteers to raise their hands as we were throughout the crowd in the yard. They told the inmates to find one of the volunteers and ask them to pray with them.

No one approached me, so I began to mingle in the crowd. Just then, I heard a very familiar voice. When I turned to see who it was, I recognized one of my bunkmates from Marion County. He had been released and was already back again. I walked up and put my hand on his shoulder. You normally didn't touch another inmate unless you knew them pretty well, so when I put my hand on his shoulder, he immediately turned to see who it was. At first, I thought he didn't recognize me until I said his name, then he embraced me.

He turned to the group he was standing with and told them I was once his bunkmate. Once the group realized that I was a former inmate, I told them that I had once worn the same uniforms they were wearing. I had eaten the same food from the chow hall and which bunk I had slept in. I could feel the hand of God on me as I witnessed those inmates that day, and nothing else mattered right then and there. My life represented a different purpose from that moment on. It was a Divine confirmation for me that day. I felt the smile of God himself looking down on me that day as if to say; well done.

Over the next few years, I would return to that same facility once more, and with that experience under my belt, I was also allowed to attend the prison that our church was serving at multiple times over the next few years. Prison ministry was a big part of my growth in this new life of mine, and I am so thankful that I followed the calling placed in my heart to go and serve the least of these.

Chapter XXXIV

Starting Over

In March of 2006, my first grandchild, Brooklyn, was born. Just like her daddy, she had that beautiful strawberry blonde hair, and I immediately fell in love with her. I couldn't help but think that had I not decided to turn my life around, I may never have had the chance even to know her.

Over the next couple of years, I kept volunteering with the media at church, and then the opportunity for a position became available for a director of communications. Anything that had to do with the worship and print media, printing and advertising. This was right up my alley. All the experience I gained with graphic design and the media experience I had volunteering at the church gave me a good chance, so I applied for the position and was hired. They already knew my background but were willing to give me the chance.

This was a huge leap for me. I had never held a job like this before. I was always the construction kind of guy, working for myself outdoors in the sun, but this was a more organized type of work that came with some big responsibilities. As a staff member, I would have a steady income, which I needed now that I was out on my own again and responsible for keeping up with the rent and utilities.

As time goes by, more and more puzzle pieces begin to fall into place along my journey. I prioritized church, and small groups were my midweek fellowship. This new routine was very helpful in keeping me focused on the positive side of life, and at the end of each day, it felt good to look back on all that had transpired and be thankful for yet another day, free and clean.

One of the things I found that I missed most was companionship. Ever since my later teenage years, I had always had a significant other in my life. It was just the kind of person that I was. I always seemed more comfortable sharing life with someone by my side. It was a prayer of mine that God would place me on the right path to meet someone special with whom I could share life.

I was a little insecure about the dating scene because of my past. I knew it wouldn't be easy to find someone to understand my origins. Yes, there were plenty of opportunities, but I wouldn't be comfortable with just anyone. I needed a partner that could understand my heart and believe that the journey that I had been on wasn't where I currently was. I didn't need a babysitter or someone to fill a void; my heart desired to find a true companion.

It was always there in my mind, but not something I obsessed over. I wasn't comfortable with the new age of dating apps, so this would have to be a different experience than anything in the past. I tried to stay optimistic, but sometimes I felt most alone, like Christmas and the holidays. At one point, I remember questioning God whether or not this was something that would ever happen again for me.

I distinctly remember the spirit of God speaking to me and telling me that I needed to learn how to love myself and be comfortable with myself before I would be ready to share that with someone else. I had never really thought of it like that. I always felt incomplete when I was single. The desire of my heart has always been to share life with someone. I didn't want to go through life alone, but God told me I needed to love myself before I could expect anyone else to love me.

That was a complete eye-opening revelation for me. I got it. It's not that I wasn't worthy of being loved again; it was that I wasn't ready to be loved again. It couldn't be a rebound; it had to be a rebirth of my

139

heart and soul. I had experienced the rebirth of my mind, but now it was time to work on my core.

In the meantime, I had an opportunity to attend a Promise Keepers event at Freedom Hall in Louisville one weekend in 2007. I had never heard of this event before, but a group of guys from our church were planning to attend, and I wanted to experience being in an auditorium with sixteen thousand men singing and praising God. What an experience! Something must be said about the echoing sound of many men singing together in acapella in an arena.

It was just what I needed. Finally, a time when I didn't have the general population watching every move that I made. A time when I could close my eyes, raise my hands in worship and let the tears finally flow. It was the first time I cried in a very long time. Years of backed-up emotions came flooding out through my tears.

For the first time, I felt free. I knew in my heart that I had been set free, but the pressures of re-entry and the temptations accompanying it had not allowed me to accept my newfound freedom and release the flood of emotions. All the guilt from the destructive lifestyle I had allowed to build up inside me was suddenly released, and I had peace in my heart again. It was very cleansing and refreshing.

This was just another step in my journey back that reaffirmed my faith. For me, this was a necessary step that I needed to take. God had placed that opportunity in front of me, and I stepped out of my comfort zone, tried something new, and came away from there knowing that I had made the right choice.

I believe that everyone's journey is different because what works for me in my recovery may not work for you in yours, but it all leads to the same place; freedom. I honestly believe anyone can receive the same freedom; you came from a different place than I did. Acceptance is key to developing a healthy relationship with God. You must believe that He is able and allow Him to guide your steps. Once you've accepted it, it's time to start living it.

Chapter XXXV

True Love

The journey has now reached the early part of 2008. I am still singing in the choir, working as the Director of Communications at the church, and performing some home inspections for extra income. I am still living at the apartment that gave me a chance. Through my faith and my new walk with Christ, I am proud to say that I never had to ask for help with rent or bills. Whenever a need arose, God always showed up with opportunities.

That doesn't mean that I walked on a white cloud everywhere I went. I am only human, and my mind wanted to question whether or not I would make rent or have enough left for the utility bills. I made it a point to thank God every night when I laid down to sleep for all that He had provided, and I even thanked Him for the opportunities that He would provide whenever I needed them.

Speaking out and thanking God for things that have not yet happened is a way of expressing your faith that He will provide. I made it a daily practice to speak positive thoughts over my life, and I still do to this day. If I say, "I'll never have enough money to make rent", or, "I'll never be able to have that, "chances are, I wouldn't. I strongly believe that positive thoughts bring positive results. Whether you believe that or not, it can't hurt to have a positive mindset.

While attending one of our weekly small group meetings, I noticed a new face in the crowd. A girl I hadn't seen there before stood out in the crowd, and I could tell she was very engrossed in the study we were doing, taking notes and very attentive. It wasn't unusual for someone to take notes, but she was different. What I saw was a young lady that was searching for more. I could see that she wasn't just there for the social life, she had a purpose for being there, and that caught my eye and made me want to know more about her.

A few weeks passed, and as I was working on some updates for the church website, I invited one of the volunteers to come to the office and look at some changes I wanted to make. She told me she was bringing a coworker knowledgeable in web design, but when they arrived, the coworker just happened to be the same girl I saw in our small group. I didn't think much about it other than, what a coincidence.

Several weeks later, I got up the nerve to introduce myself to this intriguing young lady at one of our small group meetings. I found out that her name was Christy, and apparently, our mutual friend had already filled her in on my situation. She wasn't the least bit interested in an ex-convict. It seemed all she had heard about me was the bad stuff, but that was my past, and I wasn't that person. I just had to convince her of that.

We were as opposites as any two people could ever be. While we both came from similar family backgrounds, we navigated through life on many different paths. I knew that she was a single mom of a young daughter and was recently divorced. That's about all I knew, but I wanted to know more about her. It wasn't one of those fall to pieces, head over heels, love at first sight things; it was more of an, I'd like to get to know more about you, for me anyway, because she was still not budging on any interest in me, but I hadn't turned on my charm yet.

I was eventually able to get at least her phone number, which was a huge step, and we began to text and email back and forth over the next few weeks, getting to know each other a little bit more. I'm not going to lie, I wanted to ask her out on a date, but I knew I had to keep things moving slowly so I didn't scare her away. Besides, this was very different from anything I had experienced. In the past, if someone didn't show any interest in me, I moved on, but she was different, and I wanted to know more about her.

Several months passed of just communicating through text and emails, and then I finally felt comfortable asking her out. Still, I knew it would have to be a comfortable situation for her, so I mentioned a group date to a Valentine's Day dinner that our church hosted that featured a Christian comedian. She reluctantly agreed to go as a group but clarified that this was just a fun time with friends and nothing more. I was happy to agree to her terms, and it was a great night.

We continued communicating after that night, but now we had progressed to phone conversations and became more and more comfortable with each other as time passed. I wanted her to know that my past was exactly that; my past, and that was behind me. We shared many personal thoughts, and she became more comfortable with time. She had been through a rough time with her divorce and had some trust issues when it came to men and relationships, and I understood that, so I wanted to make sure that I didn't overstep my boundaries and disrespect her.

I finally got up enough nerve to invite her and her daughter to my place for dinner. I was planning to make some chili, which was one of my favorite dishes to make. Instead of declining the invitation, she asked if I could prepare the chili and bring it to her house because that's where they both were most comfortable. I agreed, and we set a time for me to be there. Upon arriving, I met her daughter Amanda for the first time. When we sat down to eat, Amanda, about three years old, took one bite of my chili and said, "Tom, this is very delicious chili." At that very moment, she stole my heart.

On the other hand, her mother liked the chili but still wasn't sold on the idea of a 'relationship' with such a bad boy, but the friendship we were building was okay with me. I was fine with taking our time. I was more interested in proving to her that I was not the person I once was, and only time would convince her of that, and time was on my side. It didn't help that I was still on active parole during this time, but I was nearing that end in a few months, so I was looking forward to a less monitored lifestyle.

I was finally off of parole, and that felt great. Every month, for nearly four years, I had to report. I knew that there wasn't any chance of getting a dirty test, but having to report every month when I knew others that were put on unsupervised long before mine had ended was frustrating. It was like he had a reason not to trust me even when I had proven myself year after year with a good clean record, but I kept doing what I needed to do and finally finished and was officially released.

Upon being released from parole, I applied for my civil rights to be reinstated. This didn't mean that my record would be cleared; it only meant allowing me to vote. My record would never be cleared unless I could get a governor to pardon me, and I didn't see that ever happening to me. Nevertheless, I wasn't going to allow that to hold me back. I did, however, get my civil rights reinstated. All except the right to bear arms. I would never be allowed to own or possess a firearm again, even though my charges didn't involve violence or firearms.

As the journey continued, I kept noticing more and more positive achievements in my life. Even though there were some ups and downs and struggles along the way, I have noticed so many changes in my lifestyle, and I've recognized that when I continue down the right path, the outcome is so much better than ever before. I've made myself vulnerable to God's will and conscious every day of my actions and reactions that have helped to pave the path more positively.

I remember one Sunday morning while volunteering as a greeter at church, holding the door for a family; the lady touched my hand

and said, "I just love your smile so much every time I see you. How is it that you are so happy all of the time?" Do you know what that simple statement meant to me right then and there? My response to her was, "If you had been where I came from, you'd smile all of the time now too". I didn't even have to think of my response. It was as natural as the smile on my face. It felt good to know that someone else recognized my happiness for what it truly was. Not just a smile from a greeter but a smile that was as genuine as the transformation God had seen me through.

By now, the friendship between Christy and I had progressed into more of a relationship status. The fact that we started as friends and were only communicating through texts and emails in the beginning, helped us communicate more comfortably, making it easier to say some things that may not have been as easy to say had they been face-to-face conversations.

The texts and emails eventually led to phone calls, which also allowed for an easier conversation, only the phone calls were on a little more personal level. Over time, we developed a more personal relationship and began to date regularly. Christy still had a long way to go when fully trusting me, but at least we were heading in a positive direction together.

I fully understood her hesitance in trusting me completely, especially since she was a single mom raising her young daughter. It's one thing if you get involved with someone that isn't totally up front with the skeletons in their closet, but going in fully informed is another. You have a choice, and even though I don't believe that God had originally intended for our paths to cross in life, I do, however, believe that He had a hand in molding this relationship based on our hearts' intentions in the future.

I won't bore you with all the details of the relationship that followed over the next several months. Still, we found that even though we were two totally opposite personalities, we had a lot in common regarding what we both wanted and expected from a relationship. God was, and still is, the center of our relationship. Although we often fall short, as many people do in their walk with God, there is always that mutual understanding between us that our relationship is built on a firm foundation of faith in God.

Even with our polar opposite personalities, it became a healthy mix of additions to the relationship. I am more of a fly-by-the-seat-of-my-pants kind of person, and she is a much more reserved, think-this-through kind of gal, but it worked. We continued dating and eventually married in January 2009.

Not long after our marriage, I decided I wanted to renew a passion I had let go of many years ago and pursue a career in photography once again. If you remember, I had a small studio in Versailles when I lived there, but after my divorce from Laurie, I closed it and sold all of my equipment to help with the bills. At the time, I didn't have any interest in it anymore. The love for it had died, or at least I thought it had. The depression probably had more to do with it than I realized, but now, I was beginning to have thoughts of trying it again.

I started with a small digital camera and kit lenses and started taking pictures of friends and people I knew, just trying to get acquainted with the new format. Previously, I used film cameras, so the new digital technology was all new to me, and I had to start all over again. The more I photographed friends and family, the more others started asking for my services, and gradually, it became a part-time income for me.

Chapter XXXVI

The Prodigal Son

So far, you have followed me through this very long journey and probably learned more details than you would have ever wanted to, but I believe it has all been necessary for me to share every detail with you for you to experience just what I have come through on my journey back from hell.

Looking back over this journey, I can't help but be reminded of the parable in Luke 15:11-24, where Jesus tells the story of the prodigal son…

11 "There was a man who had two sons. 12 The younger one said to his father, 'Father, give me my share of the estate.' So he divided his property between them.

13 "Not long after that, the younger son got together all he had, set off for a distant country and there squandered his wealth in wild living. 14 After he had spent everything, there was a severe famine in that whole country, and he began to be in need. 15 So he went and hired himself out to a citizen of that country, who sent him to his fields to feed pigs. 16 He longed to fill his stomach with the pods that the pigs were eating, but no one gave him anything.

17 "When he came to his senses, he said, 'How many of my father's hired servants have food to spare, and here I am starving to death! 18 I will set out and go back to my father and say to him: Father, I have sinned against heaven and against you. 19 I am no longer worthy to be called your son; make me like one of your hired servants.' 20 So he got up and went to his father.

"But while he was still a long way off, his father saw him and was filled with compassion for him; he ran to his son, threw his arms around him and kissed him.

21 "The son said to him, 'Father, I have sinned against heaven and against you. I am no longer worthy to be called your son.'

22 "But the father said to his servants, 'Quick! Bring the best robe and put it on him. Put a ring on his finger and sandals on his feet. 23 Bring the fattened calf and kill it. Let's have a feast and celebrate. 24 For this son of mine was dead and is alive again; he was lost and now is found.' So they began to celebrate."

Just like the prodigal son, I was blind to everything that I had going for me early on in my life. I was more interested in the things in this world that I thought was best for me, so I turned away from everything I knew was good and set out on my journey. Squandering away everything that I knew to be good on a lifestyle that was of this world, only to be left broken and with nothing worth living for.

Longing for the kind of life I had once known as a child, I found myself at the gates of hell, ready to push through and end the years of agony and lies the enemy had convinced me to believe for so long. Clouded by the lies and destruction, I could not see any possible way out. Just when I had reached the very pit of my demise, there stood Jesus waiting to take my hand.

If it hadn't been for my parents raising us in what they believed to be the best possible surroundings, and instilled in us their belief in a greater power, and praying diligently for us, I don't honestly think that I would have come through the other side of this journey alive. I don't know that I would have known to look for Him through the clouded path of destruction. I honestly don't.

I know that some of you have followed me on this journey while reading this book and may never have had the upbringing that I had, and I know how hard it must be for you to believe that it was that easy in the end. It doesn't matter if you never even knew who your parents were; there is hope for you today.

I've seen it for myself and witnessed it firsthand in my own life and others' lives being transformed firsthand. Jesus said, *"It only takes faith the size of a mustard seed to move mountains, and nothing will be impossible for you."* Matthew 17:20

As pastor Whit once said, *"You can't go back and make a new start, but you can start today and make a brand-new ending."*

Somewhere, a parent is praying for a son or daughter struggling with addiction right now. Could that son or daughter be you? If not a parent, then a friend. If not a friend, perhaps a spouse.

Addiction comes in all shapes and sizes. Yours may not be drugs. Maybe it's something different. Alcohol, pornography, cutting, gambling, or even an eating disorder, whatever it is that eats at you daily and prevents you from knowing the inner peace that surpasses all understanding, the answer is still the same: Jesus.

As my journey begins a whole new chapter, I have been given another chance at some of the things I missed out on while struggling through life my way. I had missed out on so much of my children's childhood, and now I have been given another opportunity to experience some of what I missed out on. I was given a second opportunity to experience some of the joys of raising a small child. I had ruined the chances with my children when they were young, but now I could be a part of and enjoy watching Amanda grow up.

Joel 2:25 says, *"I will restore to you that which the locusts have eaten."* For me, this meant all of the good that addiction took from me was being restored. Since I walked out of that prison, I have always felt like I had been given back years of my life. Not literal years, but the life that was taken from me was restored. I have, and still feel, much younger than I should, given all that I have put my body through.

I'm so thankful that this is not the end of my story. God is still writing the end. I truly believe He has many more chapters to write, and I am excited to see what He has in store.

Chapter XXXVII

In Concluding

Many great things have happened during our marriage, like the marriage of my daughter Kelli to her childhood sweetheart, Aaron, in May of 2011 and the birth of three more grandchildren from my side of the family tree. TJ, our first-born grandson, is Kelli and Aaron's first child, born in October 2011. Amelia, their first daughter, was born in September of 2014, and then there was Cooper, born in January of 2020.

Some not-so-happy times as well, like the passing of my parents. They were both so instrumental in my journey. Diligent in their prayers daily for my return, and mom's relentless writing campaign while I was locked up. I am so very thankful that I had the chance to get home and prove to them that their prayers had been answered.

Dad passed away in August of 2009, and one of the greatest blessings my father gave me in life was actually from his deathbed. Yes, his life-long teachings and Christian modeling were the foundation of our family, but he left this world with a message I will never forget.

You see, he spent his last days bedridden and immobile, but even then, his testimony to the God he loved was unmistakable. In the hours before his passing, I can remember he spent a lot of time staring into the upper corner of the room with a look that was calming yet very focused. My sister asked him, "Daddy, what do you see there?" His reply was, "He's waiting for me."

Of all the things he could have ever told me about what he believed about heaven, the look on his face at that moment and his reply said more to me about heaven's reassurance than anything.

During my dad's final moments here, he spent quietly in bed with his wife and children by his side, his eyes closed, and just as his time had come to an end, his eyes opened wide as if he had seen the face of Jesus, he took one last breath and closed his eyes.

A sad moment for the family, yes, but I felt at peace for my father. I knew without a doubt that with his last breath, he had taken the hand of Jesus and stepped into eternity.

My friends, if ever one needed a reason to believe or a little glimpse of Glory, this was it. As a father, I can only hope that someday my children and grandchildren will know that the God I serve is so real and a part of everything they do.

Mom passed away from complications of congestive heart failure seven months later, but we all said she died of a broken heart. She missed her husband more than anything, and in her last days, she mentioned several times that Dad was sitting on the edge of her bed. Call it what you want, but I believe that just as Dad saw Jesus waiting for him, Mom was comforted by Dad's presence there in her last days.

Life brings with it many sorrows, but none of which shall be the end as long as we believe that we will all be reunited again someday on the other side.

At Dad's visitation, I remember seeing so many people from my childhood who came to pay their last respects. Even though it was a somber time, it was also a time of great memories with many people I hadn't seen in many years—lots of reminiscing of times past. As I reflected on that in the days following the funeral, I found comfort in many great memories. I felt the spirit of God saying that if I thought that was good, wait until I got to heaven. Peace once again flooded my soul at the thought of that. How great it is going to be when everyone is gathered there.

As the journey continued into our new marriage, Christy was provided with an opportunity to work remotely at her job, allowing us to make plans to start thinking about moving back to her hometown in western Kentucky. She had always wanted to move back home when she retired, but now the opportunity presented itself, and Amanda would be able to start middle school there. Oh, but what would I do there?

My photography business was beginning to take off well, and the thought of moving from a rural area to a small community scared me, to be honest. On the one hand, I didn't want to lose the clientele I had built up there in Lexington, but on the other hand, I felt that nudge or the prompting that God was telling me once again to trust Him. After all, as the saying goes, "You'll never be able to walk on water if you're not willing to get out of the boat."

I knew that this meant a lot to Christy to move back home to be near her family, but at the same time, I would be putting quite some distance between me and all of my siblings, not to mention I would be losing a huge part of the business I had worked so hard to build.

After much prayerful thought, we decided to put our house on the market and start planning to move to Beech Grove, Kentucky—population 294. Yep, I was convinced I would seek an early retirement and buy that rocking chair a little earlier than originally anticipated.

On the contrary, the move to this small community was one of the biggest life-changing decisions of my entire life. If you could somehow step back and see God's plan in action from above, you would have seen another one of those opportunities that I could have missed. We could have just as easily decided to stay where we were and probably would have been just fine. Still, when you prayerfully

153

consider your options, decide based on faith and trust, and follow through, you see the difference as it unfolds.

This small community has turned my lifelong dream of becoming a full-time professional photographer into a dream come true—even more than I could have ever dreamed. Before moving here, I had never experimented much with sports photography, but that is my area of expertise today. I have been doing custom sports photography for about six years, and it continues to grow. I also do some high school seniors and families, but I never thought this could ever be possible for me, especially at my age now, but God had a different plan.

While writing this book, I have had to relive some pretty tough emotions, and as I look back, it never ceases to amaze me now how God has transformed me since September 23, 2003. When this book is released, I will have celebrated twenty years free from the bondage of addiction, and I have never once regretted anything.

For those of you that have ever lost hope, given up on ever becoming anything other than the label society has given you. Blinded by the darkness surrounding you, entangled in the grips of addiction, I know your struggle is real, but today, I am living proof that there IS hope.

Jeremiah 29:11 reminds us, *"For I know the plans I have for you,"* declares the Lord, *"plans to prosper you and not to harm you, plans to give you hope and a future."*

I challenged myself to hold Him to that promise, and twenty years later, I am still reminded every day, in every way, just how far He has brought me.

May you never find the strength to give up on whatever it is your heart desires, but persevere through to the end, because it is there that you will find the peace that passes all understanding and a God who is waiting to take you by the hand and begin your new journey.

Don't forget to write your first name on the back of this book and the date you prayed the prayer earlier in this journey. If there are already other names there, write them down and be prayerful for them as you pass this book on to someone you know who might be struggling right now. May God richly bless you in your journey forward, everyone.

~ Tom

Dedicated To

To all of my siblings whom I neglected and manipulated along the way, yet you stood by my side and supported me in every aspect of my recovery, I thank you for visiting me while I was incarcerated and bringing joy to an otherwise joyless place. For bringing Kelli to visit me, praying for me, believing in me, taking me to lunch after church, and taking me to my first NASCAR race, you'll never know how much such simple acts of kindness meant to me.

To my daughter, Kelli, for never failing to let me know that I am your hero, for believing in me when I couldn't believe in myself, and for holding me to a higher standard; I can never thank you enough for your endless love. I am so proud of you for taking the risks necessary to make a better life for yourself and your sweet family.

My son, Jamie. I can never make up for the childhood you deserved, but at the time, I felt as though my decisions were with your best interest at heart. I am proud of you for overcoming so much in life, and it is my daily prayer that you never allow your past to direct your future. Keep up the good work.

My stepdaughter Amanda, who has always been as much a part of me as my own, you have given me so many memories that I may have otherwise never known. You stole my heart from a very young age, and I am so proud of the young woman you are today. Thank you for never holding my past against me and for always encouraging me to be a better man.

To Jackie and Micki, I can never thank you enough for believing in me and giving me so many second chances. Thank you for your example of tough love when I needed it most. You gave me the tools I needed to succeed and set a great example for me to follow. I hope that I have made both of you proud.

Lastly, to my wife, Christy. Thank you for believing in me. From the beginning of our relationship, you have inspired me to want to be a better person and shown me how rewarding a marriage founded on faith can be. You continually encourage me to be the best I can be and are the only reason I had enough courage to write this book.

In Memory

First, I dedicate this book to my parents' memory. Without their relentless love and never-ending prayers for me during my journey, I would likely not be writing this book today. And for their faithfulness and firm foundational upbringing, which molded me at a very young age.

To my nephew, Ben, whose journey on earth ended too soon? A very skilled and talented carpenter for such a young man. He loved working with his hands to create things for the people he loved. I never got to say a proper goodbye, but I know we shall someday cross paths again.

To Owl, the old fart that pegged me with the worst nickname a guy could think of. You had a heart of gold and a mouth that never held back what your head was thinking. I'm sorry I wasn't there to bid you farewell, my friend, but hopefully, you'll get to see ole Bait again someday. Thank you for all of the memories and laughter.

Finally, to my brother-in-law, Jackie. Even when the marriage that brought us together had dissolved, you remained a good friend. So many fond memories of the good times we shared in the shop, tinkering around and building stuff and laughing so hard that it hurt. I think of you often, mostly when I am fishing. Hopefully, you've found the blue gill honey hole on the other side and are saving some filets for me.

Prayer of Salvation

"Dear God, I know I'm a sinner, and I ask for your forgiveness. I believe Jesus Christ is Your Son. I believe that He died for my sin and that you raised Him to life. I want to trust Him as my Savior and follow Him as Lord, from this day forward. Guide my life and help me to do your will. I pray this in the name of Jesus. Amen."

If you prayed this prayer, write your first name and date in the space below. Just a first name and date you prayed will do. Then I want you to look at the other names that might already be there, and say a prayer for them. Then pass this book on to someone else that you know is struggling. With each person that reads this book, they will see your name, and pray for your continued strength.

First Name: _____ Date: _____

First Name: _____ Date: _____

First Name: _____ Date: _____

First Name: _____ Date: _____

First Name: _____ Date: _____

First Name: _____ Date: _____

First Name: _____ Date: _____

First Name: _____ Date: _____

First Name: _____ Date: _____

First Name: _____ Date: _____

7 Prayers for Addicted Loved Ones

Helping a friend or family member overcome addiction is too difficult to do alone, but God is the great healer. Here are 7 powerful prayers for addicted loved ones.

Prayer for an Addict's Freedom

Precious Savior, the powerful grip of addiction is such an apt description of sin's grip on humanity. It consumes the entire person, making it a slave to the drug. But thanks to Your saving gospel, You have broken sin's curse. I ask that You have mercy on [name] and break them free from their slavery to sin and addiction. Let the truth set their soul free, so that they may be free indeed. Let this addict's liberation be a testament to Your saving power. Amen.

Prayer for an Addict's Restored Relationships

Eternal Father, this addiction has caused a painful rift, and I pray You would fix it. Let Your Holy Spirit grant a new heart of repentance, that [name] may turn from sin and seek righteousness. Let me be discerning as to how to handle this, using wisdom and exercising grace. It would be a great blessing to see You restore the relationships damaged by this addiction. I pray in Your Son's name. Amen.

Prayer for an Addict's Strength to Resist Temptations

God in Heaven, sin has a powerful influence, indeed, and I know that none of us must take it lightly. But I also know that You are the one who conquered sin by bearing the curse on the cross at Calvary.

Sin has no dominion over You, and I know that You can supply the strength that is necessary to resist temptations. Let Your Spirit work in [name] so that addiction is replaced with Godly sanctification. May Your will be done. Amen.

Prayer for an Addict's Protection from Bad Influences

King Jesus, I ask Your intercession on behalf of [name]. Lord, please grant Your divine protection and strong embrace. Give the guidance that is needed to avoid the pitfalls of addiction and other temptations. Illuminate a path of righteousness and truth, so that evil influences will be seen plainly for what they really are. Let Your love creates a barrier of protection, and may You Spirit provide holy wisdom. Let this prayer be an opportunity for You to be glorified. Amen.

Prayer for an Addict's Daily Provision

Yahweh, You are always gracious and willing to hear the prayers of Your saints. I pray on behalf of [name], that You would provide sustenance for another day. Please allow them to survive this addition, and may it not be the cause of their own destruction. I ask that in Your mercy, You would supply safety, food, and health. Let Your continued providence be a reason that others would praise Your glorious name. I ask in Jesus's name. Amen.

Prayer for an Addict's Physical Safety

Prince of Peace, Your peace is needed in this sad situation. This addition allows danger to always lurk at the doorstep. I pray in faith that You would intercede and protect [name] from the perils that are all around. Please, by the mercies of Christ, act graciously in this time of distress. May Your saving power be on display as You show pity on an undeserving sinner. You are like a fortress of protection, and I ask You to help, in Jesus's name. Amen.

Prayer for an Addict's Redemption

God of Hope, there are many things that I could pray for [name], but the one thing that matters most is their redemption. Physical things will pass away. Food, shelter, and even health are temporary concerns. But a soul lasts for eternity. May it be Your will that this soul will not be lost forever. I pray that You would grant forgiveness of sins through faith in Jesus's gospel. Let Your mercy transforms a wretched sinner into a new creation in Christ. Please replace that stony heart with one that loves the Lord instead of sin. I praise You for Your glorious salvation. Amen.

Resource: www.connectusfund.org

Resources

Celebrate Recovery
www.celebraterecovery.com
www.facebook.com/celebraterecovery

Friends of Sinners 270-689-9174
www.friendofsinner.org

Friends of Sinners is a Christ-centered residential substance recovery program located in Owensboro, KY focusing on the restoration and reconciliation of men and women to Christ through biblical truths, accountability, and life skills. Through this, they are transforming individuals into positive contributors to society.

From Prison to Purpose
Facebook: www.facebook.com/fromprison2purpose

Harmony Ridge Recovery Center
www.harmonyridgerecovery.com

Jess's House
Facebook: www.facebook.com/jhtransitional

Connect With Us

Facebook: www.facebook.com/theprodigalsontheaddict
Email: theprodigalsontheaddict@gmail.com